E.H.T.Booth
16 May 1934

A FEW REMARKS

A FEW REMARKS

BY

ELMER ELLSWORTH BROWN
Chancellor of New York University

WITH AN INTRODUCTION BY
LeROY ELWOOD KIMBALL
Comptroller of New York University

THE NEW YORK UNIVERSITY PRESS
WASHINGTON SQUARE EAST · NEW YORK CITY
LONDON · HUMPHREY MILFORD · OXFORD UNIVERSITY PRESS

1933

Copyright 1933 by New York University

THE NEW YORK UNIVERSITY PRESS
Arthur Huntington Nason, Ph.D., Director

PRINTED IN THE UNITED STATES OF AMERICA
PRINTING HOUSE OF WILLIAM EDWIN RUDGE
MOUNT VERNON, N. Y.

IN REMEMBRANCE OF
GEORGE ALEXANDER

TABLE OF CONTENTS

		Page
Introduction	. . . .	1
I. Democracy and Democratic Education	. .	17
II. A Book of Numbers		35
An Exchange of Letters Relating to the Foregoing Essay		61
III. Imagination and Memory		71
IV. On Urbanity		91
V. Beauty and the University		115
VI. Humanistic Studies—A Forecast . . .		135
VII. Society and Solitude		145
VIII. Scientist and Artist		155
IX. One and All		167
X. The Duty of Thinking		183
XI. Dean Russell's Quarter Century . . .		193
XII. Artist Mechanics		205
XIII. Declaration and Constitution		215
XIV. Guide of Life		225
Index		239

INTRODUCTION

INTRODUCTION
Thy modesty's a candle to thy merit

THE wood-fire in the lower library of the large Georgian house which stands majestically among the elms just off campus at University Heights, burned with pleasing intermittent snappings as we pressed our suggestion. Ever faithful, quiet moving Martin put a fresh beech log on the brass andirons and disappeared through the portières as silently as he had come.

We had all been together for the greater part of two days, conversing, as friends do at such friendly sittings-around. The occasion was one of several and had become a habit of increasing frequency with the nieces and certain friends of the Chancellor during the year, and the talk had reached the subject of the academic looking piles of monographs, articles, and address pamphlets, which represented our host's unbound, and astonishingly unbounded, published activities of the past forty-five years.

"But they are all as dead as Noah!" insisted the author of the several leaning stacks of printed materials.

"But others may not think so," we parried; "and besides, if they are dead, why not give them a dignified interment under one cover?"

He laughed all over at that remark, and we thought we had gained our point, but again he winced.

"No, I could never stand it to see my past brought before my own eyes; it's appalling enough to contemplate these writings even in their present state."

"Then how about a few of those more recent ones which have caused such interesting and pleasing editorial comment?"

A FEW REMARKS

we urged, with the hope this would pierce his extreme modesty.

He made no reply, and that was to us an encouraging omen of the victory we were to experience some time later when he reluctantly capitulated. It was with the understanding, however, that the book if published should have an unassuming title.

Then came the day when we sat down by ourself, before the same busy, snapping hearth, and began the sorting process. By a series of eliminations, most arbitrary we must admit, we selected the fourteen which appear under their separate titles in this volume. No doubt some favorites have been snubbed, but what was one to do under the helpless circumstances? The selection certainly is illustrative of Chancellor Brown's catholicity and careful scholarship, even if some of the other recent ones will have to remain separately interred until such time as one is given permission, or is instructed by someone outside the family, to undertake the broader editorial function.

But to return to the leaning stacks. Halfway down in one pile appeared the light green back of what was stated to be *The Southern Educational Review*, Vol. III, No. 7, dated November, 1906. Our curiosity caused us almost to upset the others before we extracted it. On the back cover we met this statement: "*The Southern Educational Review* is doing a good work and supplying a need in Southern education— Francis P. Venable, President University of North Carolina." We turned it over, and the first two items listed in the table of contents on the front cover were: "Commissioner Elmer Ellsworth Brown . . . Frontispiece" and "The New Commissioner of Education by Professor Walter Miller, Tulane University." We thumbed with some misgivings to the frontispiece and sure enough here was a portrait, but not of the man we knew. The characteristic virility was dominant, but

INTRODUCTION

there was a black instead of a gray beard. At once we decided we liked the latest "views" much better.

We next glanced across the page to Professor Miller's article, and finished it with an inward glow, and an outward ejaculation to an empty library: Just the thing! Critical biographical material up to the Washington, D. C., days by a contemporary! *Who's Who* yielded the information that at the time when Walter Miller wrote the article he was professor of Greek at Tulane. He has been for many years past the Dean of the Graduate School at the University of Missouri. During the University of Michigan years which he mentions in the following article, he was an instructor in Greek, Latin, and Sanskrit. Some of his information had apparently been gleaned from an older brother for whom Professor Miller had a high regard. The new Commissioner of Education was thus introduced by one who had known him from Freshman to Washington:

> Nineteen years ago, when the writer of this brief sketch was beginning his first year as a teacher of Latin, he enrolled, along with about one hundred and twenty-five other Freshmen in Latin at the University of Michigan, one who, by his maturity, his many-sided experience, his serious earnestness, his zeal and energy, was at once distinguished from the other six score of that class. Between this mature freshman and his new instructor—his junior by a few years—there were many bonds of sympathy, and there soon sprang up a friendship whose ties have grown stronger as the years have gone. And in these lines the friend and the reviewer will not, as they need not, separate themselves.
>
> Elmer Ellsworth Brown was born in the stirring days of 1861, as his name suggests, at Kiantone, Chautauqua County, New York. Though the state of New York may claim him as her son, Illinois is his foster-mother; for it was in that state that he spent his boyhood, youth, and young manhood (1864–1887).
>
> Little Elmer was a remarkably precocious youngster. His letters were learned when he was but two and a half years old, and he soon showed signs

A FEW REMARKS

of becoming an omnivorous reader. By the time he was six—there was no Kindergarten in those pioneering days—he was browsing around among all sorts of books that he found about his father's house, including works on history, botany, astronomy, and physics.

He was not sent to school till he was eight years old; but, with extraordinary precocity, at the age of twelve he took the county examinations for a teacher's certificate and stood at the head of the list of competitors. No certificate was issued to the twelve-year-old boy, of course; so he went back to school. Before he was twenty, he was graduated from the State Normal University at Normal, Illinois (1881); but even before that time he had already gained two years' experience as school-master in his home state. One of these two years he served acceptably as principal of the Astoria High School.

Immediately after his graduation from the State Normal University, young Brown was appointed Superintendent of the South Side schools at Belvidere. While in this position, he manifested, even at that early age, his genius for organization. For, striking out into new paths of helpfulness through coöperation, he at that time organized the Northern Illinois Teachers' Association, and so effectually, that it has continued a successful existence upon the same foundations ever since.

By 1884 he had acquired successful experience as student, teacher, high-school principal, and city superintendent. In the fall of 1884 he temporarily abandoned the "rod and ferrule" for work very different but no less important in the many-sided preparation for the career for which he was unconsciously in training. This step took him from the training of children to the training of men; he became State Secretary of the Young Men's Christian Association of Illinois, assistant to the great I. E. Brown, his brother, one of the strongest state secretaries in America. For his own growth, it was a rich experience to be thus brought into close contact with the life and thought and needs of young men of every possible walk in life. . . .

In the fall of 1887 he became once more a student. He entered the University of Michigan as a freshman, expecting to take the full four years' course. But he had already learned to do more things in less time than other men, and he completed the requirements for graduation in two years and received his B.A. in 1889. That same summer he was united in marriage to Miss Fanny Eddy, the accomplished daughter of Dr. Zachary Eddy, one of

INTRODUCTION

the most noted preachers of Michigan, and went to Germany for graduate study. Again, with the same uncommon zeal and speed, instead of taking the usual three years to secure the degree of Doctor of Philosophy, he learned the language, completed the course at the University of Halle, wrote his thesis in German, and secured his doctor's degree within one year's time (1890).

Returning to America, he again took up his work in the profession of teaching, this time as principal of the High School of Jackson, Michigan. But before he had finished a year in that position, he was called to the University of Michigan as Acting Assistant Professor of the Science and Art of Teaching. But with such natural gifts as his and such ripeness of scholarship and richness of experience, such a place was too small for him. His success in college work was from the very start no less signal than it had been in the secondary schools. Accordingly, before the completion of his first year at Michigan, he was called to the Pacific Coast to organize the Department of Education in the University of California. It became, under his strong, tactful leadership, at once one of the most important departments in that great university, making its helpful influence felt in every grade of every public school in the state. Not only in the work of the schools did he stand for definite ideals of progress and efficiency, but for the teachers themselves he labored, and labored successfully, to make their profession as dignified as that of law or medicine and to secure their appointment, retention, and promotion on the basis of fitness alone.

His sound common sense, his practical wisdom, and his unusual administrative ability have made his counsel sought in all organized efforts for educational improvement. He has been since 1891 a member of the N. E. A. and since 1897 a member of that choice cabinet of administration known as the National Council of Education, of which he is now president. Few men in the country are serving today on more councils and boards of directors than he.

Dr. Brown has written much, and all that he has written has been welcomed. The scope of his productive activity is wide, ranging from children's first drawings to the graduate work of our universities. His *Secondary Education* was prepared expressly for the United States' educational exhibit at the Paris Exposition in 1900; and his book on *The Making of Our Middle Schools* (1903) is an accepted authority on the history of secondary schools in America. His literary work is characterized at once by clearness, force, grace, soundness of scholarship, historical trustworthiness, and persuasive reasoning. His platform addresses, which are in as constant demand as his written contributions to educational literature, are characterized by the same qualities of literary excellence and persuasive power, for he always speaks for a purpose and with the conviction of the soundness of his position.

He is, as Professor Charles Mills Gayley says, admirably summing up his professional character in the *Nation*, July 5, "not only a teacher of practical and successful experience—who has worked his way through all the grades of the American school system, from instructorship and principalship in the public schools to headship of an educational department in a great university —he is not only a practical teacher, but a scholar. His is not the superficial pedagogy of the 'faddist,' or the spasmodic procedure of the empiric. He has had a thorough training in philosophy and the history of it, in psychology and the perils of it, in the classics and the perennial vitality and need of them, in history and the unchanging fact of it, in modern languages and their efficiency in education, so far as it goes. He has the advantage of many professors of the incipient science of pedagogy in possessing an uncommon sum of common sense, in being a scholar, and a man among men as well as among teachers. He is an historian of education, versed in its relations to civilization and modern civil polity."

Personally, Dr. Brown is kind and just and true. The years he spent in the Y. M. C. A. work—a work in which his interest has never flagged—suggest the depth of his religious nature. Kindliness and gentleness are as much a part of the character as are honesty and scholarship. Our portrait of him shows a characteristic frown; but it is a frown of seriousness, not of impatience or of displeasure; through all his seriousness a rich vein of humor runs, and it is always ready to crop out in sparkling wit. In spite of all his strenuous activity and the countless demands upon his attention, he is never too busy to stop and lend assistance to the youngest and most obscure teacher in the profession or to the student seeking help; in spite of all his attainments, he is almost painfully modest and retiring; and with all his force and power and inflexibility in what he is convinced is right and for the best, he is tactful and gentle and considerate far beyond the ordinary run of men. No one will ever know how many students he has helped with advice or money or to positions after they left college. He is reserved, yet affable, high-souled, yet democratic and simple. His lovable nature and his ever ready helpfulness make all men his friends.

INTRODUCTION

Dr. Brown, now forty-five years of age, has just reached the stage of life when he ought in his new position to render his very best and most efficient service to American education. His sympathies are so broad and his practical good sense so real, that every part of the country, North and South, East and West, will in every department, from kindergarten to university, feel his quickening influence. As organizer, educator, philosopher, historian, scholar, he is eminently fitted to advance in unbroken continuity the work of our National Bureau of Education already so well begun. The same indomitable pluck that has carried him so successfully through all the changing stages of his career may be counted upon to remove every serious obstacle in the way of the highest usefulness of his new office. His judgment is steady; he is never carried away by enthusiasm for novelty, and is yet ever hospitable to new ideas that stand for true advancement; he is a scholar of many theories, but one who ever shapes his theories to the rules of practice. He is ambitious; but his every ambition is for the upbuilding and strengthening of our national character; and in the great battle of the public school for sound and effective citizenship he will prove, as President Canfield said of his predecessor, a tower of strength, standing four square to every wind that blows.

Professor Miller's reference to the wide scope of productivity before the Washington days, again started us searching the piles, and we singled out this representative group:

Die Stellung des Staates zur Kirche in Bezug auf den Religionsunterricht in der Schule in Preussen, England und den Vereinigten Staaten von Nordamerika. Halle, 1890.

Democracy in the Universities. Circular No. 3, University of the State of New York, Extension Department. Albany, N. Y., November, 1891.

How is Formal Culture Possible? The Public School Journal, Vol. XIII, No. 4. Bloomington, Illinois, December, 1893.

Children's Interest in Stories. Annual Report of the Public Schools of the City of Oakland. Oakland, California, 1893.

The Study of Education at The University of California. Educational Review. New York, September, 1894.

The Study of Children's Interest. Handbook of the Illinois Society for Child-Study, Vol. I, No. 2. Chicago, May, 1895.

A FEW REMARKS

Some Principles of Psychology that have a Bearing on the Practice of Teaching. Transactions of the Illinois Society for Child-Study, Vol. I, No. 4. Chicago, 1895.

Notes on Method in Instruction and Training. The Advance in Education, Vol. I, No. 2. Los Angeles, California, January, 1896.

The School. Tompkins School Monographs. No. 1. From the Public School Report. Oakland, California, 1895–1896.

The Selection of Teachers. From Report of the First Annual Session of the San Joaquin Valley Teachers' Association. Held at Fresno, California, October 21–23, 1897. Fresno, California, 1898.

The Appointment of Teachers. Address before the Board of Education of the City of Oakland. Oakland, California, December 6, 1897.

Notes on Children's Drawings. University of California Studies. Berkeley, California, 1897.

The Larger University Idea. Proceedings of the National Educational Association, 1898.

The High School. The University Chronicle, Vol. I, No. 5. Berkeley, California, 1898.

The Fine Art of Teaching. Educational Review. New York, November, 1898.

Art in Education. Proceedings of the National Educational Association, 1899.

One View of National Unity. The Arena, Vol. XXII, No. 2. August, 1899.

The Ethics of Teaching. From Report of the Third Annual Session of the San Joaquin Valley Teachers' Association. Held at Bakersfield, California, November 2–4, 1899. Fresno, California, 1899.

Naughty Children. (Read before the National Educational Association Kindergarten Department, July, 1899, Los Angeles, California.) Kindergarten Magazine, Vol. XII, No. 2, October, 1899.

Academic Freedom. Educational Review. New York, March, 1900.

Secondary Education. Department of Education, State of New York. (Monograph for Paris Exposition of 1900.)

Religious Forces in Higher Education. An Address Delivered at the Pacific Coast Congress, May, 1900. Pacific Theological Seminary Publications, No. 3.

Educational Progress of the Year. (A report presented to the National

INTRODUCTION

Council of Education at Detroit, Michigan, July 8, 1901.) Educational Review. New York, September, 1901.

The Baccalaureate Course in its Relation to the Professional Schools. (Read before the Department of Higher Education of the National Educational Association, at Boston, Massachusetts, July 7, 1903.) Educational Review. New York, September, 1903.

The Origin of American State Universities. University of California Publications in Education, Vol. III, No. 1. Berkeley, California, April 10, 1903.

We found in the pamphlet stacks no information of the real story of the choice of the new Commissioner, and no willing source in the subject himself; and that story of necessity will have to come from others who know the facts. A glimpse, however, into the contents of a large file convinced us that if one were allowed, one could almost build it up from the interesting letters of twenty-seven years ago from President Roosevelt and others. This glimpse, all too short, was long enough to see tantalizing old-time personal correspondence with Edward E. Hale, Benjamin I. Wheeler, E. A. Hitchcock, Theodore Roosevelt, J. G. Schurman, Edwin Markham, James B. Angell, Franklin K. Lane, Nicholas Murray Butler, Henry Suzzallo, William Loeb, Jr., Martin L. D'Ooge, John W. Cook, M. E. Sadler, Walter Miller, A. S. Draper, James Bryce, and others. Then and there we almost forgot our "introduction" for the larger field which someone will cover years hence.

The Washington years were five to a day. They began the first of July, 1906, and ended the last day of June, 1911, when the Commissioner's resignation was hesitatingly accepted by President Taft, in order that New York University might have the benefit of his outstanding educational experience. The reports for those years as presented by the Commissioner of

A FEW REMARKS

Education to the Secretary of the Interior, are contained in ten very technical looking volumes, two for each year. In addition there were issued forty-two special bulletins, representing as many special studies by experts in and outside the department. One of those which seemed to have found its way to the top of the pile read: *Facilities for Study and Research in Washington, D. C.*, by Arthur Twining Hadley, President of Yale University.

A year before the Commissioner left Washington for New York he was asked by the National Educational Association to give them a message, and there was issued, under the imprint of the University of Chicago Press, in an orange colored paper jacket, *A Message from the United States Bureau of Education* as reprinted from the volume of *Proceedings of the National Educational Association*, Boston, July, 1910. We quote here a few paragraphs indicative of the Commissioner's activities and hopes:

> Within the past year the instrument, that is, the Bureau as it may be seen from without, has been greatly changed. It has left its outgrown shell by the unresting sea of Eighth and G Streets and has entered into dignified and commodious quarters under one of the Federal Government's own roofs. It has, indeed, been taken into the bosom of the national family. Its library, which had previously been reorganized, has now been rearranged in its new quarters for practical service. A vigorous new division has been erected, that of school administration, which deals particularly with matters of interest to state and city education offices. A beginning has been made in what may be termed a field service, a service which has already engaged a good portion of the time of two specialists, those in school administration and in the work of the land-grant colleges. This service is to be further extended. Provision has been made by Congress for two important additions to the staff, namely those of Editor and of Specialist in Higher Education. The new specialist will be engaged, both at the office and in the field, with work in connection with our colleges and universities. A great campaign has recently been undertaken by friends of the Bureau with a view to the wide extension of this new service

INTRODUCTION

in the field, which promises to give us within the near future an instrument for more generous and far-reaching activities. It is earnestly desired and hoped that this campaign may meet with abundant success.

It is not generally known that this Office is equipped with one of the most extensive educational experiment stations in the world. It is an experiment station embracing some five hundred and eighty thousand square miles of territory, with two thousand five hundred miles of sea coast, sparsely populated with some thirty thousand natives of different backward races, Indian, Aleut, and Eskimo. Such a practice school presents the white man's burden in its most concrete form, with all of the difficulties and all of the inspiring opportunities presented by the world-education movement of our time. . . .

There is only one thing more to be said at this time about the strengthening of the Bureau as an instrument, and that is to refer to the strengthening of its relations with other government offices. It is true everywhere, and notably true in Washington, that an isolated office is likely to be a weak and crippled office. Among the most important steps that have been taken of late in the building-up of this Bureau have been the arrangements which have been made for close coöperation with the Library of Congress and with the Bureau of the Census. Connection with the Census Office has received especial attention during the past year. That office is now rendering invaluable assistance in the effort to secure more nearly uniform and therefore more informing statistics concerning our great state and city systems of education. . . .

This is all that it seems necessary to say at this time regarding the tool. Now, what is the larger work which the improved tool may be expected to do?

It is the business of the Bureau to collect and diffuse such information as shall help the people of the United States to establish better systems of schools. On the face of it this business would seem to be simply that of information and not that of propaganda. In a sense this is true. The office is to be a scientific office, with scientific impartiality toward the facts which it reports. But it cannot be indifferent to the facts which it reports. It must view them with reference to the improvement of our educational systems. The field in which its investigations shall be made must be selected with reference to public needs. It must call attention to the significance of the facts presented, with some positive conviction as to the directions in which there is need of improvement. It has indeed a mission. It has a propaganda. It is concerned

A FEW REMARKS

all of the time with the effort to make for this country a better education for all of the people. Some of the directions which this endeavor should take in the immediate future may be mentioned here.

We are still unable in this country to give to all of our citizens anything like a fair chance at an education. We still have some illiteracy. We still have great numbers of pupils leaving the schools before they have received a proper elementary education. There are portions of the country which are at great disadvantage as compared with others in these respects. This office of information must keep on setting forth the actual state of our school attendance, so far as it can be determined, and must reiterate the call of these simple facts to efforts for the improvement of school attendance.

The improvement of school attendance must go hand in hand with the abatement of child labor and numerous other undertakings for the general welfare of childhood. It is the business of a central office to call repeated attention to these relationships, and to help those who are at work in neighboring fields to work together for their common ends.

In a few months it will be twenty-two years since the "new Chancellor" came from Washington to New York University. To one who has enjoyed the privilege of occupying an adjoining office during those years, the time has passed much too rapidly. They have all been difficult years, each crowded with the intricate and perplexing problems of a steadily growing university. The Chancellor has faced them with energy and judgment. How well Walter Miller and Charles Mills Gayley knew their forty-five-year-old friend of 1906, and how prophetic of the years to come! "His judgment is steady; he is never carried away by enthusiasm for novelty, and is yet ever hospitable to new ideas that stand for true advancement" and "possessing an uncommon sum of common sense."

Chancellor Brown has led New York University for more than one-fifth of its hundred-year history, the longest administration of the seven Chancellors. His wise leadership and achievements had as the chief source of their inspiration, his

INTRODUCTION

gifted helpmate, Fanny Eddy Brown, who passed away January 14, 1932. Theirs was true devotion. Friends of Mrs. Brown's are building up in her name a "Collection of Modern Verse" in the General Library of the University, a collection which already runs to several hundred titles.

The wood-fire in the Georgian house among the elms just off Campus, the gathering spot of Chancellor Brown's friends, will pass to a new master. Our wish for the new, whoever he may be, is that he may endeavor eventually to become as thoughtful and as gracious a host as E. E. B. That would be perfection indeed.

L. E. K.

March 1, 1933

I

DEMOCRACY AND DEMOCRATIC EDUCATION

*Introduction to the Annual Report of the Chancellor
of New York University for the year
ending June 30, 1928*

I

DEMOCRACY AND DEMOCRATIC EDUCATION

THIS is a subject which has been written to death, but which comes to new life in unexpected ways. In these paragraphs there will be no exclusive reference to New York University, but I think they will be found to have some bearing on the problems of this university along with those of its sister institutions throughout the land.

1. As the term is here used, democracy may be defined about as follows: As related to government—the original use of the term—it is that form of government which is based on personality, apart from its attributes and characteristics, inherited or acquired. A man is to count as a man. One person one vote, no less and no more. But since government is both creature and creator of a larger social life, it is impossible to restrict the term to the areas of politics. Wherever one person counts as one, without regard for office, wealth, or parentage, there is democracy. In its lowest terms this is pure arithmetic: $1=1$.

But every man is a unit and something more, for living men have no existence apart from their qualities. It is as the bearer of human qualities that the unit is a person and counts as one. It is the man with his qualities that is of value to society. He will still count though his qualities be mediocre or undesirable, short of insanity or crime. He will count for not less than one. But in his real life he may count for a thousand, or a hundred thousand, by reason of superior qualities and great responsibilities. The qualities of men, indeed, infinitely varied as they are, tend to obscure and cancel that elemental equality. The only way that such equality can be recovered and maintained is in and through the united purpose of men who themselves are unequal and different, one from another. Such common purpose has never been realized in any large community for any length of time. We can hardly conceive of its being fully realized except as the outcome of religious conviction, conscious or implicit, attaching an ultimate sanctity to personality, whatever the cast of qualities in which it may be found.

Even where such other-world reference is wanting, however, or where it does not dominate the thoughts of men, a rising social intelligence commonly tends toward essential democracy. Human life, as such, is held sacred, legally if not morally. There is a growing disinclination on the part of the more fortunate to use their advantages to the disadvantage of their fellow men. There is also, perhaps, a vague and more or less religious regard for the fact that every man is "momentous to himself as I to me," and in some way is momentous also to the social whole. There is a desire abroad that every man shall have "a fair chance in life." The spirit of good sport accentuates this desire. Still further, there is the anticipation that lives of incalculable value to their generation may spring from the most unpromising stock and setting. A classic expression of this view is the well-known passage from Diderot's *Plan d'une université*, addressed to the Empress Catherine:

> The number of thatched cottages and other private dwellings being to that of palaces in the ratio of ten thousand to one, the chances are ten thousand to one that genius, talents, and virtue will come forth from a thatched cottage rather than from a palace.

In the main, then, the movement of human thought and practice is in the direction of democracy. It cannot be said, however, that democracy is a present fact. Rather, it is a conception, an ideal, a pious intent and purpose, save as governments of the Western world have embodied it in universal adult suffrage. Even this exception is not absolute.

2. Meanwhile, our approximations toward democracy have taught us lessons regarding human nature. We have at least begun to learn that there are no "masses." We have found that every class and condition of humanity is shot through and through and crisscrossed in every direction by influence, leadership, control, which emanates from diverse personalities and is made manifest in all manner of dominance and deference.

Every man is both leader and led. His range may be of the lowest and narrowest, but if he be not actually defective some other looks to him to lead in some petty concern or employment. His range may be of the highest and widest, but even so he must have advice in many fields, and because of his superior intelligence he relies the more upon competent direction in fields and subjects which he has not himself mastered. The head of a state has his trusted and official counselors; but beyond that circle he is under the social guidance of his wife, takes orders from his physician, follows his guide in the northern woods, and may be as clay in the hands of his tailor.

No leader and no follower can escape altogether from this network of relationship. All must in some measure learn to lead, all must in some measure learn to pick and follow their leaders. Free leadership, freely chosen and freely changing, is of the essence of democracy.

The point last indicated is often overlooked: that the supreme test of a leader may lie in the choice of those whom he will follow. As a leader, he influences others to join in the same following. If he trusts a newly risen star in the field of science, it may be, or of policy regarding the open shop, or of diet, or of healing, or of interior decoration, or of soaps or cigarettes, others will lean in the same direction. If he holds by some older allegiance, others will share in his conservatism.

It follows that in all of its developments mature democracy is of necessity a representative democracy. Every genuine leader makes choice of other leaders and adds something of his own in the making of that choice. The addition that he makes may be of supreme importance. In any case, the advance of knowledge in these days renders it imperative that governments, elected on the democratic principle, must devolve great areas of governmental action upon trustworthy agents, of commanding competence in their several spheres of action. It is only by so doing that they can justify the confidence that the people have reposed in them. Such delegation of responsibility—government, representative in the second degree—must advance with advancing knowledge if universal suffrage is to hold its own as a governmental procedure.

3. This, with little alteration, will be recognized as of that simon-pure democracy which flourished in the thought of the eighteenth and more or less of the nineteenth century. Its unbounded idealism, its romanticism, and other imperfections not a few, have been unsparingly exposed in the present generation; but as the bed-rock of individualism it has been the point of departure for thought of a more social character which has succeeded it; and the thought of other generations will, no doubt, return to it from time to time for fresh departures. Its educational implications are obvious:

That all citizens should have opportunity for education up to the level of their native abilities;

That all should have opportunity to discover themselves and be discovered as regards their special aptitudes and abilities, and should receive the training appropriate to their varied endowments;

DEMOCRACY AND DEMOCRATIC EDUCATION

That all, according to their capacities, should have opportunity to acquire the general competence necessary to an appraisal of their fellow men, as regards those concerns of life in which they must have the guidance of others; that, being followers, they may not be blind followers;

That in so far as their abilities and experience fit them for leading, they shall come to understand the responsibilities of leadership.

It is plain to see that, much as we fall short of the democratic ideal in modern society, we fall short of that ideal still more conspicuously in modern education. But progress is making. Artificial hurdles are lowered one by one, or removed. Adult education is on the way to becoming universal: in time we shall come to regard it as a normal development, and not as something exceptional and incidental. Our psychologists and sociologists are making tentative advances in "vocational guidance," but only tentative as yet. Finally, democracy itself is slowly learning the need of real education, and is less receptive than it was to sham and superficiality bearing the democratic label.

4. With the later nineteenth century and the earlier years of the twentieth have come those social interpretations of democracy which dominate the thought of the present time. The idea was discovered—rediscovered rather, with apparent surprise and enthusiasm—not only that a man grows into a coöperative creature, but that there was a "co-" about him from the beginning. If he survived his babyhood and childhood, it was because others, already established in their group connections, provided him with food and shelter. From first to last, he was institutional or nothing.

The giving and receiving of influence, leadership, control, of which each individual is undoubtedly a center, are seen then to be rarely if ever the force of one personality playing upon another, singly and alone. Back of all is the concentrated energy of the many acting as one. Families, gangs, unions, professions, lodges, casual groups, political parties, industrial and commercial corporations, institutions of religion, of the arts and sciences: in bewildering interaction, they sum up and reinforce and complicate the human energies in operation in any given personality at any given moment. The freedom and range of personal leadership in a democratic society encourages the growth of such associations. The most of them are ephemeral, but some of them gain speedily a militant coherence, with every promise of endurance, while some of them have endured for ages. All of them, old and new, are subject to challenge and to incessant change, *intra* as well as *inter*.

We find that the more permanent of these institutions, continuing from generation to generation, provide stability, where unorganized democracy would tend to become uncertain, fluid, volatile. They are centers of conservatism; at times they are centers of ingrained and ineradicable prejudice.

We find that the less permanent, or at least the newer, of these groups provide opportunity for unusual initiative and leadership to make itself immediately effective. They are centers of progress; at times they are centers of demagogy and mob-psychology.

Prejudice, widely shared, on the one hand, and the contagion of impulse on the other hand, are the dangers to democracy which are bound up with the innumerable groupings characteristic of our social life. While they are dangers from opposite directions, not infrequently each of them plays into the hand of the other.

5. A people, then, with which democracy is concerned, is not merely an aggregate of individuals. It is not merely an

aggregate of personal centers, receiving and dispensing influence and control. Beyond all this, it is a society of colossal human organizations, transcending and overpowering the strength of any individual: shadowy at times and remote, at other times terribly present and inevitable; now coöperating one with another, now in unconscious or open conflict, but all of them pursuing ends which seem to them good, and many of them directed with full purpose to the furtherance of the general good.

They seem like over-personalities, in which the lesser personalities of men and women are swallowed up and threatened with extinction. In what sense and what degree they are real personalities is the subject of unending debate in the fields of theoretic politics and jurisprudence. The literature of this discussion is of the greatest interest for those who are concerned in the philosophy of public affairs, ranging as it does from the most uncompromising atomism and nominalism to deliberate fiction and the verge of mysticism. But leaving that aside, it is clear that education in a democracy is preparation for life in and among these titanic existences.

What kind of education is to prepare men and women to live out their lives, fruitfully and without disaster, in this terrific companionship, which at one moment tramples upon them and at another moment lifts them high, as partners in tremendous undertakings and participants in universality?

6. The most obvious answer to this question, the immemorial answer, is that education should prepare directly for those connections and activities in which chiefly the life of the one educated is to be lived: his economic life and his spiritual life first of all, apprenticeship for his trade or profession, catechism and dogmatic instruction for his higher faith and loyalties.

A FEW REMARKS

At their best these methods have been effective. In one form and another they have their permanent place and use. But democracy finds them inadequate, for democracy is concerned with the man, as a living unit, and not merely as a fragment of an institution or as a cog in a machine. For democracy, then, a man is to be educated for his group-life, plus. And in this case the *plus* is primary in importance.

7. Men must be trained, and trained with unsparing discipline, for the trade or profession by which they are to rise above a life of idleness and gain a livelihood and rear a family. To belittle such training is either sheer blindness or academic snobbery. But where such training is too narrowly practical, it defeats its chosen purposes. An artisan who is only an artisan, a doctor who is only a physician, a school-teacher who is only a schoolmaster, does not last. He breaks down in an emergency. He is a temporary asset who becomes a liability. So the man must be trained while the artisan is being trained. The man must be educated at the same time that he is preparing for his profession. In other words, liberal education is not to be limited to schools and colleges of liberal arts, but the technical and professional schools must likewise educate liberally. If in pursuance of this ideal they send out graduates less expert in the beginning than those more narrowly trained, a little slower to mature in their chosen occupation, we shall not be unduly critical of such graduates, provided that they give evidence of a solidity of educational grounding, a substance of personal character, and an intelligent outlook upon the world of ideas. But the view that the liberal and the professional are mutually exclusive is misleading. The better teaching of a profession is inevitably liberal.

8. So far, the economic; then what about the spiritual life, among men so absorbed in institutions? The life of an insti-

DEMOCRACY AND DEMOCRATIC EDUCATION

tution is in the allegiance and loyalty of its membership. It is through their allegiance and loyalty that it gives back life into their lives and into the life of the world. Their allegiance and loyalty is confirmed by ideas, and these ideas take shape in creeds, declarations, platforms, philosophies. As has been said, the systematic teaching of the ideas which an institution embodies has always had its place and usefulness. To this day young men and women who have been brought up under a well-defined moral code, with its social and religious sanctions, have an advantage over those whose moral conceptions have been chaotic from the beginning. The Ten Commandments, the Sermon on the Mount, the Westminster Catechism, one or two or all of them, have been a point of departure for lives which have achieved the highest personal independence and influence. But here again democracy finds the transmission of fixed and final forms insufficient.

It is well-nigh impossible for any individual to live his life in a single institutional relationship. He is the child not only of his family but of many another foster-parentage, religious, political, economic—whatever they may be. They grip his mind and his affection with varying authority. Their diverse claims upon his life are bound to clash from time to time. His morals are disciplined through his response to these opposing demands. He finds a certain freedom in balancing and harmonizing his discharge of obligations in several relationships, whereas if his whole life were given to one of these relationships to the neglect of every other he would be in slavery. His internal conflict, answering to the wider competition of interests in society at large, will rise at times to violence and tragedy, involving all of the powers of a man in intellect, feeling, and will. Through this interplay and warfare of their institutional faiths and loyalties men discover and reveal their individuality, the essential force and quality of each of them. On the other hand, through the part they play in this everlasting interchange, institutions are themselves remade from generation to generation. But to attain to this freedom and influence, a thinking man must not only break away from enslavement to any one institution. He must, at least in some degree, break away from subservience to institutions. In some degree—a small degree at best—he must rise above them, so that he may see them in perspective. He must at least endeavor, with the old philosophers, to see his world and himself *sub specie æternitatis*.

So we find that the institutional view of democracy brings us back after all to the individual as the unit of our educational effort—the same old unit, with new emphasis and new meaning. If all men are to influence and be influenced, control and be controlled, not only as related to other men but still more as related to dominant groups of men—corporations, parties, churches, and all—then they should be braced for their part with the best discipline which each of them can appropriate and use. At every stage of their education they must be liberally educated.

9. Two great aspects of liberal education, humanistic and scientific, are both of them essential to the liberalizing of education even in the professional schools. In medicine and engineering, for example, pure science is readily finding its place; but the need of the humane elements, historical in the wider sense, is not so generally recognized. In schools of theology these proportions are presumably reversed.

The college of liberal arts comes again into its own in this view. The connection between the rise of modern democracy and the rise of modern science has been pointed out by numerous writers. Science will have the truth without regard for personal preference. So far as it holds to this determination, it may be regarded as democratic; so far as it departs from it, it ceases to be scientific. Science provides man with weapons and tools by which to master the physical world through knowing it and changing it. But inductive science alone will not liberate the individual. Unless he knows the social cosmos into which he is born, he will be bound down by his own lack of adjustment. Here history is his dependence—the humanities, history in the large—while history even in its narrower meaning is the appropriate introduction to any science and to any profession. I should be inclined to stress this point. To get his bearings in any science or in any profession, a student requires some knowledge of its place in human history.

But all knowledge is in process of growth. To transmit it as a rounded finality is as unsatisfactory as to teach by rote a compendium of faith or morals, "mere powerless information," as Pasteur called it, "instead of a science of progress and futurity." Under competent teaching, college students see knowledge in the making and continuously in the making. To that end, our college teachers must themselves be participants in that endless operation of widening the range of knowledge. Herein appears the need of higher studies in our institutions of learning, for the research and training for research which commonly centers in the graduate school. It would be impossible to measure the value, to a democratic society, of teachers and teaching that are alive with that untiring pursuit of knowledge and more knowledge.

10. In the next place, more than ever, from a democratic point of view, education seems destined to be a concern of the state. It is not to be forgotten that it is the modern state, the nation, that has given the first and only comprehensive embodiment of the democratic principle, in the form of universal

suffrage. It is to the interest of the state that the electors should exercise this right with high intelligence and integrity. In the conflict of social institutions at the present time, the state is subject to challenge, perhaps the bitterest challenge of all. The stream of change meanwhile is affecting both the ordinary operations of government and the fundamental conceptions of sovereignty. Here we have to do not only with operations within a single nationality, but with the activity of organizations wider than any single nationality. These confront us on every hand. Ancient dreams of universal empire, political and spiritual, are taking on new life. The wider intercourse which modern science has effected is giving them new stimulus and expectation. The newer aspects of the economic interdependence and solidarity of mankind have assumed an extraordinary significance. Patriotism has come to be discounted in many quarters as provincial and outworn, while for these critics internationalism and world-unity are the order of the day. Nevertheless, in spite of all shortcomings, the state today, with its component political units, is actually the main reliance of men for the redress of flagrant inequalities, and is still the supreme earthly object of their devotion. To those who prefer to regard the state as only one of many corporate entities within its borders and one that is declining in relative importance, this simple statement will seem a simple exaggeration. So far as this country is concerned, however, it cannot be questioned in any seriousness.

An autocratic government, perhaps of necessity, gives to education the character of propaganda. A classic example is that found in Taine's account of education in France under the first Napoleon:

> He assigns to himself the monopoly of public instruction. . . . "In the establishment of an educational corps," he says to himself, "my principal aim

DEMOCRACY AND DEMOCRATIC EDUCATION

is to secure the means for directing political and moral opinions". . . . In this way, . . . Napoleon becomes in fact the sole head-schoolmaster of all Frenchmen, . . . the unique and universal educator in his empire.[1]

Governments nominally democratic have not been free from this taint. Notorious cases will be recalled in which American governments, State and municipal, have interfered with the management of public schools and universities for partisan purposes. But, making allowance for all lapses, these claims for our American practice may be generally sustained: that it perseveres in providing public education that is liberal in character and not narrowly propagandist; that it provides still farther for free opportunity, both individual and institutional, by fostering schools and colleges under other than governmental control; and that it maintains a healthy state of public opinion by freely educating its own severest critics.

From one point of view, democracy may be regarded as a way of dealing with the incessant change which goes with human association of every kind. A democratic state is one that unreservedly commits its destinies to the public opinion of successive generations, and in each generation trains up the next not simply to carry forward a tradition but to form its public opinion independently, in the light of competent intelligence and knowledge, both historical and scientific.

11. Taking the long look into the future, however, it must be clear that the ultimate hope of democracy lies in an organized world, in which every human unit shall count as one and have its own fair measure of opportunity: a world "safe for democracy" and a democracy safe for the world. That is remote, but steps in that direction belong to our own time. The point to be emphasized here is that the approach to that end, the orderly and hopeful approach, must be chiefly through

[1] *The Modern Régime*, translated by John Durand, Vol. II, ch. 2.

national channels. The impatience that would discredit the nation as a hindrance to an all-embracing humanity will not make for the secure advancement of democracy. Nevertheless, democratic education in all of its stages, and the more insistently the higher it goes, must take account of our rising citizenship in that larger world of humanity. This is preëminently true of universities. Democracy and modern science are together bringing a fresh vindication of the original prerogative of universities; namely, that they shall cultivate universal knowledge, as *scholæ orbis terrarum*.

12. But still further, the fact cannot be overlooked that a religious element in some sort inevitably enters into the spread of democracy. That elusive equality which lies at the heart of democracy, hard to define and impossible to dislodge, carries intimations of something beyond. Equality and fraternity hold together, and neither of them can hold without some measure of feeling, and of faith. Scientific regularity may discard that something beyond because of its vagueness, and religious regularity may seek to reduce it to a form, but in any case it goes on doing its work as do those rays of the sun that are invisible to human sight. Meanwhile, universities, in their endeavor to understand the forces actually at work in human societies, cannot disregard the study of this religious element, whether in its formlessness and diffusion or in its historic and institutional embodiment.

13. We hear certain American universities characterized from time to time as distinctively democratic institutions. I think it will appear from the foregoing paragraphs that any university that is true to its name is democratic in the better sense of the term, and that any institution that has not in it the democracy of sound learning is not worthy of the name *university*.

DEMOCRACY AND DEMOCRATIC EDUCATION

In education, however, as in politics, the terms *democracy* and *democratic*, as well as their contrasting terms, are so broad and vague as to be easily misleading. The interpretation of democracy in education which I have suggested above would make of it a discovery of leadership in its countless grades and varieties and institutional relationships, a development of leadership for the general as well as for an individual good. But what are genuine leaders but the *aristoi*, and what is such a system of education but the making of a genuine aristocracy? It does not greatly matter then what designation shall be applied, but it does matter above all that our leaders shall be liberally educated.

14. If anything of value in these paragraphs is found to be a far-off echo of Plato or Milton or Newman or Matthew Arnold, or of Emerson or Thomas Jefferson, I shall enter no denial. But I am indebted also to recent publications, not a few. Of these let me mention one of the latest, the volume on *The Pragmatic Revolt in Politics* by Professor W. Y. Elliott of Harvard University, which came from the press this summer, after the greater part of the above had been written. I have found the book extremely interesting and stimulating.

Let me pay tribute here to the memory of another to whom I have long been indebted in many ways, Richard Burdon, Viscount Haldane, whose death a few weeks ago brought a painful sense of loss to many men and many associations of men. A member of the British nobility and twice Lord High Chancellor of the realm, he was conspicuous for his democracy and for his promotion of democratic education. A man of vast learning in many fields, notably in jurisprudence and in speculative philosophy, his practical statesmanship was manifested in distinguished services as minister of war. With the

A FEW REMARKS

outbreak of the World War, the *demos* turned against him as a friend of Germany, a frenzied outbreak which drove him for a time from public life. Meanwhile the military command acknowledged the incalculable service which he had actually rendered to the national defense. For his own part, he returned serenely to his studies in German literature, no less a patriot that learning was for him unlimited by national boundaries. Some years earlier, as head of a parliamentary commission, he had made an exhaustive study of the problems of the University of London. The report of the Haldane Commission, while some of its chief recommendations failed of adoption, stands as a landmark in the history of education in a democracy.

In making personal acknowledgment of the New York University report of last year, Lord Haldane expressed his interest in what was said of education in an urban environment, making particular mention of passages on adult education and military training, and went on to say that the report "adds to one's faith in the development of higher education in your great country. You are fortunate in having so many rich men who are . . . also keen idealists."

II

A BOOK OF NUMBERS

Introduction to the Annual Report for the Year ending June 30, 1930

II

A BOOK OF NUMBERS

LET me call attention to certain features of American higher education in the broad and large. I do this because it seems to me that this University, or for that matter any university, can the more surely find its appropriate place and function, if its governing officers and its faculties shall view its concerns as part of one great and dominant concern of the American people.

One aspect that has commanded attention everywhere is the rapid increase of student attendance. Salient facts regarding this increase for the country at large are the following, as reported by the Federal Office of Education:

> In the year 1900 the total enrollment was   167,999
> In 1910 it was 266,654
> In 1920 it was 462,445
> In 1928 it was 868,793

These figures represent students enrolled in universities and colleges for the regular year. If students of collegiate grade in teachers colleges, normal schools, summer sessions, and extension and correspondence courses are added, the total for the year 1928 (the latest for which full statistics are available) rises to 1,325,675.

A comparison by percentages is still more striking: from 1900 to 1928 the population of the United States (continental territory) increased 58 per cent; while in the same time regular university and college attendance increased 417 per cent.

If one approach the situation from another angle, it appears that in 1900 the number of these regular enrollments was equal to 2.85 per cent of the total number of persons of the normal age of college attendance (years 19 to 22, inclusive); in 1928 this percentage had risen to 11.77, or if we include the numbers in the other institutions of collegiate grade, to 17.95 per cent. One may well hesitate to say that all of these will have had the "higher education," but unquestionably the most of them will have had some exposure to the direct influence of the higher education in some one of its American forms, and a great part of the number have received, or will in due time receive, university degrees. These facts call for serious consideration.

1. The figures cannot be fairly interpreted without a consideration of the attendance upon our public high schools, for even in the Eastern States, with their historic fitting schools, the high schools now furnish the bulk of our university attendance.

In the year 1900 our aggregate high-school enrollment was	519,251
In 1910 it was	915,061
In 1920 it was	2,199,389
In 1928 it was	3,911,279

While the total population increased (from 1900 to 1928) 58 per cent, and university and college attendance increased 417 per cent, high-school attendance increased 521 per cent.

One who travels about this country will find these bare statistics strikingly confirmed by the rapid upgrowth of impressive buildings for high schools, some of the most notable of them for junior high schools; while friendly talks with household servants, day laborers, wage earners, or their employers, will reveal the family pride which centers in boys and girls who are already "in high school." In certain states, New York among the number, compulsory school-attendance laws reach up into the high-school age. After making due allowance for students who fall out by the way, one cannot but be impressed—if not appalled—by the swelling tide that is continually overflowing from these high schools into our colleges and universities. It is reported that forty per cent of our high-school graduates proceed to college or to some other institution of collegiate grade. Some estimates run as high as sixty per cent. Here in the city of New York alone, 21,746 boys and girls have received diplomas of graduation from the public high schools of the city in the past year. Of these, the number who are looking forward to college and university studies may be guessed from the fact that of the graduates of the past two years nearly seventy per cent have gone on to the higher institutions. A like situation appears over the whole area of some of our western states. The old familiar lines seem addressed directly to our higher education:

> See a long race thy spacious courts adorn;
> See future sons, and daughters yet unborn,
> In crowding ranks on every side arise,
> Demanding life . . .

Our educational realists will find the demand for "life" entering into the situation in disconcerting ways, with a fine lot of ironical implications; but no one who knows the situation can doubt that in all of this is to be found a genuine demand for a larger life.

2. The saying of Thomas Huxley regarding an educational ladder, with its foot in the gutter and its top in the

university, "by which every child . . . might . . . reach the place for which nature intended him," has been so often repeated that it has become trite, but it has unquestionably had its part in the making of our educational ideal. In the educational systems of the mid-western and Pacific states, dominated by their great state universities, this conception has been realized to an extent that Huxley could hardly have foreseen. But the same ideas and purposes have long been making their way in our American universities under the forms of private as well as of public control. We had been setting up the educational ladder, or something better, East and West and South, before Huxley's saying had become current in this country.

3. Another Englishman has more recently put forth another saying which is likely to be often repeated as the twentieth century proceeds in the development of national systems of education. In 1917 Mr. Herbert A. L. Fisher, then newly appointed president of the English Board of Education, now warden of New College, Oxford, laid before Parliament his first education estimates in a speech of unusual significance. Mr. Fisher's personal connections with this country, as lecturer on the Lowell Foundation in 1909 and 1924 and as orator of the Boston tercentenary in July of this present year, lends for us an added interest to his words. When he spoke in his tercentenary address of the "forward-reaching vision of destiny" disclosed by John Adams, who "thought about great things in a great way," he spoke as a kindred and understanding spirit.

At the outset of his presentation of the education estimates, Mr. Fisher humorously referred to his speech as "the first quavering utterance of a new member." In its closing paragraphs, he declared with no uncertainty, "I . . . see my way clear to a really systematic and many-sided development of the organism of public education. . . . The object which we are all striving to attain is very simple. We do not want to waste a single child. We desire that every child in the country should receive the form of education most adapted to fashion its qualities to the highest use. This will mean that every type and grade of school in the country must be properly coördinated." The legislation initiated by Mr. Fisher in pursuance of these purposes marks one of the most notable forward movements in the history of English education.

It is interesting to note, by the way, that among the members who complimented Mr. Fisher on his "first quavering utterance" was one whose name has become more familiar in recent years, Mr. Ramsay MacDonald. Mr. MacDonald declared that "this is the first time that we have had any evidence of a real attempt to unify and dignify our educational system." He criticized Mr. Fisher's treatment of secondary education as not even approaching finality, but went on to say, "The right honorable gentleman did not talk about the education ladder. That is a great blessing. I hope that it is decaying and rotting, and is about to disappear wholly. But he did talk of the education highway, which is a very much better term."

"We do not want to waste a single child." Every child shall "receive the form of education most adapted to fashion its qualities to the highest use." The saying is pithy and portentous. If we in this country should adopt it as unreservedly as we adopted and amplified the idea of the education ladder, we may find it leading us into undertakings that tax the imagination. And how can we fail to adopt it—if we have not in effect adopted it already? It calls up a glowing picture of a nation in which every citizen from the beginning of life is regarded as an invaluable asset, to be conserved and developed up to the full measure of his capacity to contribute to the general good. The education offered to every one is to match the measure and variety of his ability, whether native or acquired. He is to have, even beyond Huxley's dream, the opportunity to "reach the place for which nature intended him." This would mean that society at large should have, in full development, a personal composition such as nature has "intended."

It may not be amiss to have called up this vista which Mr. Fisher's words suggest, for, while it reaches far out beyond anything that is now in sight, it indicates the direction in which we are moving. The prospective cost of such a program would be staggering, if any cost could stagger the American people when they believe the returns will exceed the outlay. It would carry up into the highest range of education the homely saying of Booker Washington, "It will not pay to allow any portion of our population to remain uneducated."

4. But now, what portion of our population is really capable of pursuing an education into the higher studies? Not all, certainly. The majority, we must believe, fall short of the mental capacity to rise into these exacting pursuits. What percentage of our people, all other considerations aside, could under ideal conditions attain thereto?

Here we are on the ground of genetics, and it is slippery ground. One school of psychology claims that the differences among men are chiefly hereditary—that the place of every child, in the scale and the variety of his mental capacity, is already fixed at birth. On the other hand, the social psychologists have shown that supposedly hereditary tendencies are often due to the subtle working of social heredity, in the child's earliest environment. I am here an innocent bystander of a psychological mêlée, though possibly not altogether innocent.

A BOOK OF NUMBERS

At least it seems clear that supposedly native abilities are elastic. We may admit that there are bents and limitations that are inborn—hard to define and manifest only in reactions to environment, material and social; but the educational influences of early life, chiefly those outside of the schools, have been shown to have an effect hardly less than creative in the making of mental faculty. A mind that has come up from infancy in an atmosphere where ideas are not taboo, where books, science, culture, college, slip in casually and naturally in the daily talk of the family circle and acquaintance, is likely to meet the demands of higher education with less of awkwardness and effort than one whose intellectual life has been dulled and depressed from the beginning. As families and communities become pervaded with influences from the centers of higher learning, as bachelors of arts and science become more numerous and less exotic, the numbers of those who in their later teens will show at least a freshman grade of intellectual ability may be expected to advance.

It may be noted in passing that the controversy regarding heredity versus education has recently received attention anew, in Professor T. H. Morgan's monograph on "The Mechanism and Laws of Heredity," which appears as the first chapter of that voluminous work, *The Foundations of Experimental Psychology*,[1] edited by Professor Carl Murchison. The chapter is accompanied by a bibliography of 217 titles.

5. One is reminded here of the controversy between Mr. Walter Lippmann and Professor Lewis M. Terman which enlivened the pages of *The New Republic* in 1922 and 1923. Mr. Lippmann declared that "the claim that we have learned how to measure hereditary intelligence has no scientific foundation," but admitted that the measurements of the psychol-

[1] Clark University Press, Worcester, 1929.

43

A FEW REMARKS

ogists were likely to prove of use in other directions. This controversy, an echo of the one which had long gone on and is still going on in the field of scientific psychology, grew directly out of the report by Messrs. Yoakum and Yerkes in their book entitled *Army Mental Tests*.[2] These army tests undoubtedly constitute the only attempt that has ever been made, or perhaps ever could have been made, to take stock of the man-power of this country as regards the various grades of intelligence available for public use at a given time.

Writing on this subject for *The North American Review* of June, 1921, I spoke of the results of the army examinations as follows:

> These figures would indicate that from twelve to fifteen per cent of our male population of the ages represented by the draft have the mental capacity to pursue a college course. Strictly speaking, they prove nothing as yet, for the tests are still in a provisional stage, which calls for revision and redirection. But they lend weight to the surmise, based upon a general review of the field, that the number of our citizens who could pursue advanced studies with profit to themselves and to the community is far greater than the number now enrolled in our colleges. We may at least estimate that eventually something over ten per cent of our adult population will be equipped with education, in some one or other of its forms, above the high-school grade, and that our industries and professions will require and will absorb this output of highly trained men and women; or that at any given time not less than one per cent of our total population will be enrolled as students in higher institutions of learning. It seems not unlikely that this proportion may be realized within the next twenty to thirty years, if the tendencies already well established shall continue their sweep, undisturbed by new world currents or by national disaster.

It is now evident that these estimates were conservative. More than one per cent of our total population is already enrolled in institutions of learning of a grade beyond that of the sec-

---

[2] Henry Holt and Company, 1920.

A BOOK OF NUMBERS

ondary school. One would hesitate now to estimate the numbers of our adult population who within the next generation will have enjoyed some measure of such advanced education, at less than twenty per cent, or to name any limit with the expectation that it will be immutable.

This peering into the dim future has an obvious bearing on certain questions that are asked from time to time, relating to the present situation and the years immediately before us: Is our American society approaching the point of saturation, as regards the percentage of its numbers to be found in attendance upon our higher institutions of learning? Have we not already reached the limit, "passed the peak," and must we not expect a stabilized ratio or perhaps even a retrogression in the immediate future?

For the reasons given above, I look upon the limit, psychologically considered, as altogether indefinite. Not only is it true that more students are going to the universities today than were going a generation ago, in proportion to population, but it is also true that more students in proportion to population are capable of pursuing university studies. It may be that we shall reach a stabilized ratio for other reasons, but not, in the near future, for lack of mental capacity in our people.

6. On the other hand, are we nearing the point of saturation as regards the number of highly educated men and women whom the industries and professions can absorb and utilize; or, better, as regards the number who can find suitable employment with a happy adjustment of their abilities to their social milieu? This is a complicated problem, which calls for objective and scientific study. It cannot be answered by any simple formula; of that we may be sure. Any provisional answer must take account of the rapid changes now going forward, and the probabilities of a rapidly changing future. I

A FEW REMARKS

can only stress at this point the importance of such an inquiry, particularly in its bearing upon capital expenditures for teaching and research, and make a few brief comments in passing.

Some centuries ago, it was a question how large a part of the population might be taught to read and write without disturbing the social equilibrium. Now our occidental societies have been placed on a platform of universal literacy. Any problem of social adjustment might now be expected to arise at the upper end of the scale. Of this, Germany presented an example some twenty and thirty years ago, when there was much talk of the dangers of an "educated proletariat," referring to the holders of university degrees who had become so numerous that many of them could only with difficulty find employment that would yield the barest livelihood.

We have had no such danger to face in this country, thanks in part to the absence of social stratification, in part to the wider range of studies offered in our universities, leading to a wider range of occupation in life. In certain professional fields, however, the relation of demand to supply has been the subject of serious investigation by the General Education Board, the Carnegie Foundation, and other privately directed organizations.

Attention should be called to a recent publication of the National Industrial Conference Board, *Public Education as Affecting the Adjustment of Youth to Life* (1929). This little volume was prepared with the assistance of an advisory committee of eighteen members, made up about equally of men of industry and educators, assembled by the National Industrial Conference Board under the chairmanship of Mr. Howell Cheney. In the words of its preface, it

portrays briefly the economic and social conditions that have most influenced our educational system and are now surrounding it, and outlines the accomplishments of the system, as well as the major criticisms which have been most forcibly leveled at it. No attempt has been made to initiate or conduct researches . . . but . . . to indicate in which directions research seems most needed and may be of most value, in the interest of the individual, of industry, and of society as a whole.

The concluding chapter of the book presents proposals for such researches. An appendix lists the agencies of educational research that are now in operation. While this preliminary survey directs attention chiefly to the earlier years of adolescence, the middle teens, it is significant for the higher education as forecasting the nation-wide surveys and researches that undoubtedly await our American colleges and universities in the not-too-distant future.

Many pages might be devoted here to the increased demand, in the industries and in business, for men who can meet and deal with the newer scientific developments, which are cropping up everywhere and taking even alert executives by surprise: the growing demand for men who can appreciate and utilize scientific research; for men who can train subordinates to manage instruments and processes the full meaning of which they cannot readily master. These trends, however, have been so voluminously discussed by others that I will not enlarge upon them here. I think the need of objective and many-sided and long-continued inquiries along these lines is apparent.

7. For reasons given above — the elastic character of "native" intelligence, the elastic demand for such intelligence when adequately trained, our ingrained purpose to give every citizen his chance, the flood of candidates pouring forth from our high schools — for all of these reasons put together, I cannot anticipate any general recession in the numbers of students in our higher institutions, but see rather a likelihood

A FEW REMARKS

of further increase. We may, however, look for some slowing down of the recent rate of increase.

But while we do not want to waste a single child, and with this intent are pushing them on to the highest education of which they are capable, we are becoming conscious of waste in other directions, the waste of maladjustment. We refrain from assigning to each young citizen a predetermined place and occupation, as might be done under a communist or fascist régime, but we have become acutely aware that in shaping his own destiny he needs all of the light that society can throw upon his way. Accordingly, "vocational guidance" and related activities have come into prominence within the past decade, with all of the mechanism of mental measurement that can be devised in furtherance of these ends. Our foremost universities are offering courses and providing systematized advice of this general character. It would be hard to name any development in our higher education since the World War more prevalent and characteristic than this. The number of organizations, institutions, and publications within this new field of cultivation is already bewildering. . . .

These brief notes give the barest hint of the extent and ramifications of an undertaking that is spreading through our secondary schools and universities with a rapidity which one is tempted to compare with the spread of miniature golf in this year of 1930. It has, to be sure, its aspect of fashion and faddism, and its more intelligent practitioners are keenly aware of its comparative ineffectiveness hitherto. Some of its most substantial gains are doubtless those in which psychiatry is its chief ally. But psychiatry, too, is painfully feeling its way, and its relations with educational guidance may be mutually advantageous. The defects of the endeavor at guidance at its present stage must not close our eyes to its fundamental importance and necessity. If we are to go on beckoning this vast company of adolescents up into the highest education of which they are capable, we must give them any help that can be given towards finding their place in a world of men. While avoiding the waste of uneducated abilities, we must seek to escape the waste of misdirected education.

The fact of chief significance in the present discussion is that the decade 1920 to 1930, which has seen the most amazing increase in college and university attendance, has been equally characterized by this widespread and courageous endeavor to overcome the treatment of students as in a mass and to give them due attention as individuals. Those who are disposed to think that our universities, particularly state institutions and those in great cities, are taking in vast numbers of students indiscriminately, should know of the many-sided effort that is making to sift and assay these multitudes, for their own good, the public good, and the good of the institutions concerned.

This involves, moreover, the endeavor in many directions to give our more highly gifted students both stimulus and opportunity to make the most of the gift that is in them. Universities that have now grown large are apparently doing more for these more promising students than they were doing when they were middle-sized institutions twenty or thirty years ago. These efforts may well be quickened by an acute anticipation that the years before us will make extraordinary demands for leadership of the highest quality trained to its highest capacity.

8. Hitherto, I have barely touched upon aspects of this problem of numbers, any one of which might well occupy a volume of concrete studies and the interpretation thereof. But let us turn now to certain moral aspects of the whole situation,

which seem to me highly and indeed supremely important.

To give our citizens the largest opportunity not simply to acquire but to achieve is of itself a moral concern of large significance. It fires the ambition of individuals to become what they believe themselves capable of becoming. But not every one to whom the opportunity is offered will seize upon it or appreciate its value. The opportunity itself tries out the character of those to whom it is offered; and with the opportunity should come whatever education can give towards the strengthening of character in those who lay hold upon it.

More specifically, students in the later high-school years and in the freshman year of college should find that the successful pursuit of the higher studies depends not only upon intelligence but upon moral stamina as well. If the student has not the honesty, the industry, the persistence, the self-control which such studies rightly demand, he is not to find or keep his place in the happy environment of college and university.

This means that the higher education should make the higher demands, and should not be regarded as higher education at all if it does not make those demands. The piling up of what President Eliot called "short information courses," does not carry a student forward into higher education, any more than the mastery of the tricks of a trade or a profession. The difficult step to what may fairly be called higher is not simply an advance in knowledge but an advance in the power and method of mastering knowledge. Language and critical comparison for the humanities, mathematics and systematized observation, experiment, and verification for the natural sciences, coherent thought and interpretation for both, with such administration of the curriculum that only intellect and will combined can pass its portals: these conditions are necessary if our higher education is to test and to invigorate the moral quality of its students.

Two comments should be made here in passing: First, the pleasant paths of academic culture are still to be found and should be found in our universities, but they should be open to those only who have proved their competence in the severer studies which will render culture substantial and significant. Can we not do this and still find a thought and a way for the exceptional student whose path to creative usefulness and glory lies above our rules and regulations? Secondly, the rejection of students either before or after entrance upon collegiate studies must not, save in extreme cases, be of the nature of a separation of the sheep from the goats. The rejected are still members of civilized society, and are entitled to all possible guidance in finding their own best place and function in society. Incidentally it may be noted that while seventy-three per cent of those whose names appear in *Who's Who in America* are college and university graduates, another eleven per cent is made up of those who attended but for one reason or another were not graduated. There is left no inconsiderable remnant of those who made their way without help or hindrance from academic disciplines.

9. There are larger moral issues to be considered. Society owes its overcrowded and laboring universities an adequate and discriminating support; they in turn owe to society a reinforcement of all that makes for righteousness. These obligations are accentuated by the fact that society, with its increasing admixture of graduates, will more and more be shaped and re-created by their influence.

If universities in general held to a creed or code, if they were instruments of propaganda of a prescribed system of ethics, it might be possible to evaluate that system and weigh

A FEW REMARKS

the social good or ill resulting therefrom. Even that would be difficult. But where college men differ so greatly in their views, their convictions, and their partisan alliances as is now the case, that difficulty seems an impossibility. Can we, indeed, fix upon any definite moral good which society has a right to expect from the higher education or which does in fact accrue from that source?

All depends upon the quality of college and university teaching. For this reason, if for no other, the maintenance of the teaching staff of these institutions at their highest level of character and ability, at this time of vast expansion in numbers, must be a chief concern of the nation at large. In so far as teachers and teaching are at their best, our higher education may be confidently expected to show tangible results in the moral realm. For the young men and women so trained, the conception of truth will be a ruling principle in all relations of life. They will have learned to look for truth, regardless of private interest or prejudice. In some measure, they will have learned that other and larger lesson: to see the truth of any present situation in its wider bearings, its background, its tempering and interpreting history, its humanity. They will have learned to shun the falsity of unrelated truth. In both general and professional studies, in all departments, sound teaching involves a full measure of this ethical soundness, this implicit propaganda of moral values. It makes, moreover, for an intelligent acceptance of that basic principle of social welfare, that the good of every individual is bound up with the good of his community and the good of the community is bound up with the good of its individuals. This principle only high intelligence can advance from the stage of Kipling's

> For the strength of the Pack is the Wolf,
> And the strength of the Wolf is the Pack,

to the stage suggested by President Theodore Roosevelt's

> This country will not be a good place for any of us to live in if it is not a reasonably good place for all of us to live in.

So university teaching, at its best, even apart from its express teaching of philosophical ethics, makes inevitably against an unsocial and sordid individualism on the one hand and social regimentation or mob-rule on the other. Between these extremes lie the countless possible adjustments to each other of society and the man, in which the great movements to the making of a better world are to work themselves out in the years to come. If, as between the two, university studies tend towards a preponderant emphasis on the individual, on personal cultivation, personal rights, and personal responsibilities, such an incidence of emphasis can well be defended as wholesome and necessary, in order that the mass-consciousness of an unthinking humanity may be in some measure redressed.

What manner of man must a teacher be, who is not stirred at times with a thought of the moral hazard and moral promise which any competent teaching in college or university carries with it! That thought is intensified many fold by this impact of vast numbers of students, to be taught by an increasing number of college teachers. Out of these numbers there will certainly emerge great teachers swaying the development of great students, here one and there another, through whom the new and unknown world before us is to be organized, liberated, spiritualized; while for a far greater number, academic freedom—no longer remote and mysterious—will become a daily accompaniment and stabilizing factor of all other freedom, in all grades of our social organization.

10. In another place, I have ventured to refer to such an effect as "government by influence." A conception similar to

this finds highly suggestive expression in certain writings of George Holmes Howison, a philosopher whose philosophy has no adherents in these days, but whose teaching, none the less, has been a bridge from nineteenth- to twentieth-century thought in some eight or ten American universities, whither his students have gone as professors of philosophy and psychology. Following Aristotle, but only in part, Howison writes of his own system that "It reduces efficient cause from the supreme place in philosophy which this has hitherto held, and gives the highest, the organizing place to final cause instead." He exalts that supreme government which "reigns . . . not by the exercise of power, but solely by light; not by authority, but by reason; not by efficient, but by final causation."[3] In human affairs, it goes without saying, a government by light without power would be no government at all, but here again the trend of government as affected by the wider spread of higher education is a subject for thought. As Howison added, with his penetrating insight into the interaction of personalities, "The created, as well as the Creator, creates. . . . Freedom that freely recognizes freedom is universal." This is pure idealism, but pure democracy is pure idealism, with all of the dangers, the contradictions, the enthusiasms of idealism.

We may pass over the historic expression of such idealism, but we are not to forget that government in these days is bound to make increasing use of many forms of knowledge, rigorously determined, and of norms and motives of conduct implicit in such knowledge. Herein lie chiefly the animating ideals of democracy, or of any other -cracy that is modern in spirit. Wherever they seep into the common life of our people, there is hope.

[3] *The Limits of Evolution*, Macmillan, 1901.

A BOOK OF NUMBERS

11. It follows that our teaching faculties of the higher studies must become education-minded in a broader sense than that concerned solely with the problems of individual students or of individual institutions. They must look before and after over the whole life of our people, which they are inevitably remaking. They must survey, criticize, and amend their own contributions to that life, in the light of a consistent educational theory and purpose. They must overhaul their pedagogy of instruction, to meet the requirements of large classes, coming from all manner of social antecedent and environment. They must become aware of their part, along with that of other institutions, in the discharge of a nation-wide and nation-deep responsibility—to say nothing as yet of a still more inclusive responsibility. They must become, in their spiritual unity throughout the land, the chief organic agency in the shaping of the America that is to be, at least so far as its conscious aims and ideals are concerned.

In actual fact, one of the significant movements sweeping through our universities along with this great inrush of students is a fresh endeavor to view our higher education in its relation to the general welfare. There are so many indications of this trend that it is difficult to select representative examples. I may refer, however, to a few with which I have been particularly impressed.

One of these is the conference of colleges and universities held at the University of Minnesota in July, 1927. The papers presented at this conference were published in a volume, edited by Earl Hudelson and entitled *Problems of College Education*.[4] In an introduction to this volume, President Hopkins of Dartmouth makes use in a striking manner of Robert Louis Stevenson's analogy between life and the shadow

[4] University of Minnesota Press, 1928.

A FEW REMARKS

of a great oak. After the familiar quotation from *Lay Morals*, President Hopkins goes on to say:

> So it is with education. The accurately drawn figure of a given moment may be descriptive of little existent in the next. The relation of shade to light alters continuously from year to year. It is consequently incumbent upon the university, from time to time, as frequently as possible, to examine the figure it has drawn of what education is and often to make revision of its concepts of what its own artistry must portray.

This publication, along with a number of others issued in recent years, confirms the opinion that the University of Minnesota is now one of the important centers for a university study of university problems in their broader implications.

For three years in succession, the University of Chicago has held an Institute for Administrative Officers. With the third session, that of 1929, began the publication of the *Proceedings* of this Institute.[5] The fourth session, held in July of this year, presented a program of broad interest, in which leading educators from many institutions participated.

Purdue University, under President Elliott, established a Division of Educational Reference in 1925. This division now publishes a series of *Studies in Higher Education*, which, while having immediate bearing on the problems of Purdue, have also a wider interest, and have commanded attention in colleges and universities throughout the land.

Ohio State University has the distinction of having put forth this year *The Journal of Higher Education*, a monthly magazine, of which Professor W. W. Charters is editor. This is, I think, the first regular periodical we have had in this country devoted altogether to the interests of higher education. Such a journal had long been needed. The Division of Higher Education, erected in the Federal Office of Education at

[5] Gray, Dean William S. (ed.), University of Chicago Press, 1929.

A BOOK OF NUMBERS

Washington in 1910, has been rendering good service in the collection and distribution of information through occasional and annual or biennial reports, but there was still the lack of a vehicle for the frequent and continuous interchange of views and information as between colleges and universities. In supplying this lack, the new journal is rendering a valuable service.

The latest annual report of President Angell, issued in February of this year, is a particularly interesting document, in its emphasis upon the coöperative study of university problems by the several faculties of Yale. Its introductory paragraph is significant:

> I doubt whether any great university was ever so consistently and uniformly concerned to improve its methods of procedure as the Yale of our day. Even institutions which, at this point or that, are more or less in intellectual ferment commonly possess considerable areas over which appreciable inertia, or self-complacency with the *status quo*, are obtrusively in evidence. There have certainly been periods in Yale history when that was true of her. But, with equal certainty, it is not characteristic of our time. To be sure, the changes which have been thought essential, or advisable, are much more radical and thoroughgoing in some parts of the institution than in others. But everywhere there is active interest in fundamental educational problems and policies, everywhere there is thoughtful and well-considered experimentation in progress.

Speaking in more general terms, President Angell goes on to say that

> The universities as the repositories of knowledge and truth, and the guardians of the discovery of new truth, as well as the trainers of the intellectual leaders of each new generation, must be incessantly alert and open-minded to apprehend promptly and discerningly what is happening in the world and how education may adjust itself to altering circumstance.

In the universities mentioned, and in many others, there is now going forward a consistent effort to relate the activities

A FEW REMARKS

of the single institution to aims and conceptions which are at least nation-wide. In one form or another, those engaged in the daily tasks of education are studying its fundamental problems, with some apprehension of the fact that these are virtually identical with the fundamental problems of human society in its whole organization.

It is a significant fact that educational institutions are not alone in shouldering this responsibility in national leadership, but that American industry is disposed to assume some share of the burden. Reference has already been made to the tentative entrance upon the study of education in the earlier years of adolescence by the National Industrial Conference Board. In the field of the higher education, the alliance of the Institute of American Meat Packers with the University of Chicago is important and promising. In addition to other features of this coöperation, it has culminated from year to year in a series of annual conferences, notable gatherings which bring together many of the foremost leaders in both industry and education for fruitful discussion. Six of these conferences have now been held and the seventh is appointed to meet in Chicago in October of this year.

12. New York University has for years past had its part in these studies of the more general problems of higher education. In the year 1915 a series of conferences was initiated, at which representatives of the several faculties met for the discussion of problems fundamental to all university instruction. In my annual report for the year 1916–1917 appeared the following paragraph:

> In an autocracy, the schools may be used to hammer and weld a people into the character which will effectually serve the ends of an imperial government. In our America it is no less imperative that the national character shall be impressed upon the schools of the land; but here we have the more difficult task of educating, not for mere solidarity, but for freedom and the respon-

sibilities of freedom. . . . The adjustment of instruction to the strangely interlocking activities of general and professional education, and to the need that both forms of education shall be a preparation for public service as well as for private advancement, indeed the whole effort to make higher education serve the higher needs of the nation, now calls for greater pedagogical skill and insight than has hitherto been demanded of college instructors. Not only must our schools for the training of teachers be raised to the highest pitch of efficiency, but university faculties, to a greater extent than is now common, must become agencies for the study of the educational situation of the country, and must devise and recommend measures for meeting the country's educational requirements.

In 1926 a department of higher education was erected in our School of Education. Meantime, the other schools of the University were carrying forward self-surveys under faculty committees, and informal groups from related faculties were considering not only common problems of administration but also the theoretical questions underlying those problems. In my annual report for the year 1925–1926 I said:

> It will not do that universities be centers, chiefly, of educational tradition. They are called to be centers of educational thought. . . . A matured and inclusive and advancing wisdom is required of the teaching profession today, to the end that the nation may be, essentially and morally, the gainer and not the loser by the new momentum which is entering into the advancement of learning. . . Universities have before them a mighty task of sheer educational thinking, if they are to meet and master this world of change.

We may take a certain pride in the fact that this University, as it rounds out its first century and plans for its second, is not only carrying its part of the responsibility for the education of large numbers of our citizens, but is continually taking thought for the bearing of its teaching upon needs of American life, both economic and spiritual, and seeking to lessen the human waste that is incident to the massing of great numbers in a great new social experience.

AN EXCHANGE OF LETTERS RELATING TO THE FOREGOING ESSAY

AN EXCHANGE OF LETTERS RELATING TO THE FOREGOING ESSAY

THE MASTER'S LODGINGS : UNIVERSITY COLLEGE : OXFORD

3d December, 1930

Dear Chancellor Brown:

I have read with deep interest and some excitement your Annual Report which reached me from Mr. Busse today.

All over the world one feels the weight of American example, of which one of the most striking characteristics is the trend towards almost universal higher education. You in the United States have been the first to give scope to these new aspirations on a magnificent scale. Other countries, not least those of the East, are following your lead, with varying degrees of delay or inhibition due partly to psychological, partly to economic obstructions.

I am glad that you think that the structure of the United States is elastic enough, and the economic possibilities vast enough, to absorb the ultimate product of this colossal movement. In the work of American engineers and others in foreign countries one sees the overspill of what you have already produced.

I find that in Germany there is alarm at the numbers of the academically trained who are temporarily unemployed. But emigration, though less free than it was, may provide an outlet of considerable help.

Pushed to the extreme, the doctrine of securing for every one the education for which the individual is fitted by talent and character would, I think, invite state control of all occupations and the direction of individual ability into the channel of education, or, subsequently, of employment deemed best by superior authority in each separate case. But questions of cost will put on the brake before this consummation is achieved, though it seems likely that in some countries attempts will be made to trench deeply into capital in order to secure educational opportunity and employment for those educated, largely at the public expense.

Believe me

Yours very sincerely,

(*signed*) M. E. Sadler

The Chancellor
New York University
New York

NEW YORK UNIVERSITY
OFFICE OF THE CHANCELLOR
WASHINGTON SQUARE
NEW YORK

23 *December,* 1930

Dear Sir Michael:

I am keenly interested in your letter of December the third and am gratified that you found my statement regarding the numbers of students in American universities worthy of such penetrating comment.

The question of the interrelations of supply and demand promises to be of prime importance in both the economic and the academic field for a long time to come. In the economic field, it is intimately wrapped up with the problem of distribution. In the academic field, there will, undoubtedly, be a

AN EXCHANGE OF LETTERS

similar implication. In both fields, we are slowly coming to the practical acceptance of the world, rather than the nation, more narrowly considered, as the unit of our vision.

But whether for the nation or for the world at large, the disturbing question remains, whether the balance of supply and demand must eventually be determined by Government, which would resolve itself into autocracy, or may still be accomplished by the free determination of individuals, working through agencies other than those of Government, which would offer a hope of continued democracy. Possibly representative government, working in general harmony with the free organization of citizens, may still offer a hope of continued democracy, but the balance is difficult. Certainly, by some course or other, the number of citizens receiving the higher education must be rationally related to the changing needs of society.

But may I venture another question which may, in its implications, be even more disturbing: Are our modern societies, through education for society, proceeding towards a situation in which the terms will be reversed, and society will, to all intents and purposes, function and exist for education? These speculations may well make us a bit dizzy, but they are rather forced upon us by the course of events.

Just now, in the practical field, a reassuring thing is happening under our very eyes here in the city of New York. Under the utterly unprecedented avalanche of unemployment, the city government is making a practically forced contribution from all city employees for the direct relief of actual want; while, at the same time, and in full accord with the city government, a voluntary committee of citizens has, within a few weeks, raised a contribution from all classes of society amounting to more than eight million dollars, for the specific purpose of providing temporary jobs for heads of families who are out of work and in actual distress, and these jobs, in parks, hospitals, and other institutions of a public character, are distributed by four permanent and experienced agencies of relief, of a wholly voluntary character. At latest report, over twenty-one thousand of such heads of families were employed, each for three days in the week, at a wage of five dollars a day. It is one of the most extraordinary and stirring exhibitions of the adjustment of a democracy to an unprecedented crisis which we have ever seen. . . .

Very sincerely yours,

(*signed*) ELMER ELLSWORTH BROWN

Sir Michael E. Sadler
The Master's Lodgings
University College
Oxford, England

THE MASTER'S LODGINGS : UNIVERSITY COLLEGE : OXFORD

5th January, 1931

My dear Chancellor:

I cannot refrain from sending a few lines of thanks to you for your most interesting letter of December 23d. Your account of the effort which is being made in New York to help the unemployed is very stirring and shows how ready the American people are to rise with generosity to the urgent needs of a crisis.

Your question whether modern societies, through education for society, are moving towards a state in which society itself will mainly function for the purpose of education is very

AN EXCHANGE OF LETTERS

stimulating to thought. It reminded me of the chapter on "The Stationary State" in J. S. Mill's *Principles of Political Economy*. You will remember that he said that "a stationary condition of capital and population implies no stationary state of human improvement. There would be as much scope as ever for all kinds of mental culture, and moral and social progress; as much room for improving the Art of Living, and much more likelihood of its being improved, when minds cease to be engrossed by the art of getting on." Mill thought that the great development of mechanical inventions had not yet begun at that time (1848) "to effect those great changes in human destiny which it is in their nature and in their futurity to accomplish." He looked forward to a time when "in addition to just institutions, the increase of mankind shall be under the deliberate guidance of judicious foresight." Only in that case, he thought, could "the conquests made from the powers of nature by the intellect and energy of scientific discoverers become the common property of the species, and the means of improving and elevating the universal lot." Mill was evidently thinking of the world as a unit. The stationary society, the coming of which he thought he foresaw, would evidently apply education (in the widest sense of the word) to people of all ages with a view to enhancing the common good.

But he would certainly have disliked a rigid society, in which individual energy had no scope for effecting industrial and social changes. A balance between control and liberty seems the true aim. But in the rhythm of change there is rather violent reaction between the two poles. In Great Britain, at the moment, control is stronger than individual enterprise except, very significantly, in the Arts and in Literature, which are a symptom of a coming change. I conjecture that the

A FEW REMARKS

expenditure on education and social benefit made by any one nation will be levelled down by economic forces if they rise too high above those established in other countries which are their inevitable competitors in the exchange of goods. But great economies are possible without impairing the real excellence of what is now being done for public education and comfort. The satisfaction of freedom is much too deep for us to submit (except as a temporary medicine) to complete control on all sides of our life. And if we, in England, have to take this medicine, I hope it will not be for long.

With kindest regards,

Yours very sincerely,
(*signed*) M. E. SADLER

The Chancellor
New York University
New York

NEW YORK UNIVERSITY
OFFICE OF THE CHANCELLOR
WASHINGTON SQUARE
NEW YORK

10 *February*, 1931

My dear Sir Michael:

I think it clear that we have a common hope and purpose; namely, that the rising stream of those receiving the higher education, instead of being confined within limits by governmental control on the one hand, or allowed to spread wastefully over the land on the other hand, shall be intelligently self-directed in ways that shall make for the good and the betterment of human society.

AN EXCHANGE OF LETTERS

With renewed appreciation of your stimulating contribution to the discussion of this question, believe me

Very sincerely yours,

(*signed*) ELMER ELLSWORTH BROWN

Sir Michael E. Sadler
The Master's Lodgings
University College
Oxford, England

III

IMAGINATION AND MEMORY
Introduction to the Annual Report for the Year ending June 30, 1929

III

IMAGINATION AND MEMORY

SPEAKING of a college executive, a recent writer has said:

> Perhaps it is an artificial distinction to separate the educator and his theories from the president and his work, but where so much the larger proportion of annual reports must be concerned with details of administration, purely educational addresses and articles give a clearer picture of the theories and the visions underlying the work of administration.

In the case of a large and many-sided university, it seems to me, on the contrary, that the educational outlook which gives something of perspective and coherence to the whole is an essential part of the report. To tell the dream and the interpretation thereof is as important as to count the fat kine of gifts and bequests and the lean kine of academic hunger. In recent years, I have accordingly prefaced my reports with some general views which have seemed to me pertinent. In pursuance of this practice, let me speak at this time of a tendency in our twentieth-century education in which New York University has its part along with other institutions. I refer to a general shifting of emphasis from memory to imagination. I think the study of this movement will help to a better understanding of New York University, particularly in its more recent development.

The change referred to in this bald characterization is a veering away from the mere amassing of knowledge to knowledge in its use and interplay, as growing and creating; from precept to discovery and invention; from tradition to an acceptance and expectancy of change. It appears in a height-

A FEW REMARKS

ened respect for the individual student and his choices, as over against that standardized mass-production which is supposed to dominate our educational procedure. It calls for a new rapport between teacher and student. It renders teaching a more interesting and exciting enterprise for both.

1. The modern age was ushered in by a great awakening of the imagination of the Western world, and this awakening was for a time reflected in the teaching of a few influential schools. I find myself reading again and again a notable little volume on Renaissance education which I first read some thirty years ago. It is by William Harrison Woodward, sometime professor of education in the University of Liverpool, and is entitled *Vittorino da Feltre and Other Humanist Educators*.[1] The author of this book has put forth later works on the teachers of the Renaissance, which are familiar to students of the history of education, notably his *Desiderius Erasmus*; but in both subject and treatment his *Vittorino* has a peculiar charm.

Vittorino da Feltre, who conducted a famous school at Mantua for many years, down to his death in 1446, is called "the first modern schoolmaster." He was, in fact, more than a schoolmaster in the common acceptance of that term. It was said of him that he "was perhaps the first to prove that humanism had not only made possible, but indeed demanded, a new ideal of a teacher of youth."

It is pleasant to turn from those temperamental aberrations of other scholars which marred the rise of humanism to this high-spirited teacher who steadfastly directed the study of the classics to his one great purpose in life, the development of "the complete citizen." He gave his attention not only to the literary side of education but also to the physical and the

[1] Cambridge University Press, 1897.

IMAGINATION AND MEMORY

spiritual, in full faith that the classical and the Christian tradition, and the courtly tradition as well, could work together to a common end. He won for himself and for his ideals the devoted adherence of his prince, his pupils, and his learned associates. The list of his friends is impressive: the Gonzagas, father and son and other members of the ruling family; Vergerius, Barzizza, Guarino, George of Trebizond, Theodore Gaza, John of Aleria, Ambrogio, and how many others! Leading names of that great generation in which Greek first took its place alongside of Latin in humanist education, and Latin first shook itself altogether free from medieval limitations. "His relations . . . with those scholars with whom he came in contact were of singular friendliness. . . . It was impossible to quarrel with Vittorino."

So we find in him a foremost representative of that group of enthusiastic teachers who with the new learning brought new life into the fifteenth century. They turned to the past with an imagination which magnified its glories and overlooked its imperfections. The minds of their pupils were indeed stored with the treasures of a mighty literature, which they sought to imitate; but none the less their chief concern was for the future, for the making, in their own age, of a nobler civilization.

I have dwelt upon these beginnings for we are here at the fountain head of more than four centuries of modern education. It is good to recall the freshness and vitality of the best Italian schools in those earlier years. Something of that freshness and vitality passed over into the north of Europe in the century following. In England we find it in Colet and Sir Thomas More, and in their itinerant friend and idol, Erasmus.

How this morning glow was dimmed in the centuries fol-

A FEW REMARKS

lowing need not be retold at length. It is the old story of pedagogic atavism: after the *Grammarian's Funeral,* a narrower grammarian and then a narrower yet; Ciceronian dogma; whole generations of schoolboys painfully memorizing their Lily; Sallust for exercises in parsing; Ovid and Vergil for vowel quantities, with verse composition to fix those quantities in the memory. One classical revival after another made the attempt to recapture that first rapture. Meanwhile, in spite of the worst that the schools could do, those serene and glorious literatures of the ancient world went on teaching their unfathomable lessons to a chosen few in every generation.

2. We come at length to the nineteenth century, to the later decades of the nineteenth century. What a different learning kindled up the imagination of that new age, what different modes of thought! To this day we can hardly measure the depth of the transformation. It appears most conspicuously in the natural sciences and in industry, and in those great inventions which bind science and industry together. Everywhere, imagination at its busiest, and education slowly awakening to the spirit of the age.

John Tyndall's address on the "Scientific Use of the Imagination" (1870) is still the classic in its field. It rises in places to an eloquence which we in this day find the more impressive because of its restraint:

> There is in the human intellect a power of expansion—I might almost call it a power of creation—which is brought into play by the simple brooding on facts. The legend of the Spirit brooding over chaos may have originated in a knowledge of this power. . . . Philosophers may be right in affirming that we cannot transcend experience; but we can, at all events, carry it a long way from its origin. We can also magnify, diminish, qualify, and combine experiences, so as to render them fit for purposes entirely new. Urged to the attempt by sensible phenomena, we find ourselves gifted with the power of forming mental images of the ultra-sensible; and by this power,

IMAGINATION AND MEMORY

when duly chastened and controlled, we can lighten the darkness which surrounds the world of the senses.

Tyndall and the mighty group to which he belonged had hardly passed off from the scene, in the nineties, when there began that new development in physical science, associated with the names of Roentgen, Curie, Einstein, Rutherford, Bohr, whose work called for a violent enlargement of the scope of scientific imagination—an enlargement that brought growing pains to the scientific world, in which the unscientific world must participate, though it be ever so vaguely.

3. For the present purpose, I pass over the vast, pervasive influence of the evolutionary philosophy and the more obvious educational changes of the nineteenth century—the enrichment of the curriculum, the growth of school and college laboratories, and the like—and come to one change that is more central to this discussion. I refer to the freer election of studies by college and university students.

The immemorial endeavor to build a national culture upon an established unity of intellectual pursuits, in virtue of which all educated men should understand one another, had plainly begun to give way. In this country, Harvard had already been making tentative moves in the direction of freedom in the choice of studies. But a conservative reaction had for some years been dominant in Harvard when Charles W. Eliot was called to the presidency of the College. That conservatism still prevailed during the early years of his administration. But his own desire and purpose to carry freedom of election to the farthest extreme was forecast in his inaugural address in October, 1869:

> For the individual [he said], concentration, and the highest development of his own peculiar faculty, is the only prudence. But for the state, it is variety, not uniformity of intellectual product which is needful.

A FEW REMARKS

He spoke with unusual fervor of the meaning of free election of studies to the individual student:

> When the revelation of his own peculiar taste and capacity comes to a young man, let him reverently give it welcome, thank God, and take courage. Thereafter he knows his way to happy, enthusiastic work, and, God willing, to usefulness and success.

In other institutions the same leaven was working, though few of them went to the length to which Harvard was finally led. Nevertheless, the fixed curriculum for all was a thing of the past long before the close of the nineteenth century; and the disposition of students to shape their own education and the disposition of college faculties to follow them rather than lead has furnished readable copy for the newspapers in more recent years.

4. The new age soon found interpretation in a new philosophy. William James issued his little volume on *Pragmatism* in 1907. He wrote as follows:

> The term . . . was first introduced into philosophy by Mr. Charles Peirce in 1878. In an article entitled "How to Make Our Ideas Clear," in the *Popular Science Monthly* for January of that year, Mr. Peirce, after pointing out that our beliefs are really rules of action, said that, to develop a thought's meaning, we need only to determine what conduct it is fitted to produce: that conduct is for us its sole significance. And the tangible fact at the root of all our thought distinctions, however subtle, is that there is no one of them so fine as to consist in anything but a possible difference of practice. . . . This is the principle of Peirce—the principle of pragmatism. It lay entirely unnoticed by any one for twenty years, until I, in an address before Professor Howison's philosophical union at the University of California, brought it forward again and made a special application of it to religion. By that date (1898) the times seemed ripe for its reception.

Probably no other philosophy has so quickly influenced educational thought and practice. This is owing in part to the

IMAGINATION AND MEMORY

interest of William James in schools and schooling; and far more to the intimate relations in which our other leading pragmatist, John Dewey, has had with the schools and teachers of this country and of foreign countries for the past thirty years and more. Pragmatism, through all of its variations of name and content, has been almost equally and simultaneously a philosophical and an educational doctrine. Its educational influence has, moreover, worked upward from the elementary schools into the high schools and colleges rather than in the opposite direction. It is only of late that it has really begun to affect the colleges, though finding there older elements with which to fuse and coöperate.

The fact that is chiefly germane to the present discussion is that, wherever its influence has spread, this current doctrine has discountenanced the teaching of any fixed form of truth or precept, regarded as a finality. It has laid an emphasis never before equaled upon the initiative and constructive purposes of the learner. Sheer repetition, rote, imitation, formation and information—they are at their lowest in this school of thought, while imagination, as initiative and creative activity, is at its zenith.

Of the many books which express this general view, I may mention those of Professor Hughes Mearns (*Creative Youth*, 1925; *Creative Power*, 1929), which are representative in their individuality. The following passage is from the first named (page 28):

> The only chance the world has, so many think in all parts of Europe and America today, of breaking its old bad habits and forming new good ones is by fostering—not thwarting—the impulses of youth. The new education becomes simply, then, the wise guidance of enormously important native powers.

A FEW REMARKS

The change of which I am speaking is wider than any formulated philosophy. It has in it the buoyancy and confidence of youth, a faith the more daring as it escapes formulation. Education has in a way declared its independence. It refuses to serve simply as an agency of other institutions: for the hammering in of their doctrines, political, religious, or any other, or for the teaching of anything whatever by mere rote and memorizing. It is assumed that education itself, conceived as the furtherance of self-education, is the chief and ultimate concern of human society.

5. It is plain to see that this has in it seeds of revolution, but not of revolution as the overturning of an old system by a new system. It is as much against Marxianism by rote as against monarchy by rote or democracy by rote. Here is not organized revolution but chaos. In much the same way the seeds of revolution and of chaos were in the teaching of the Renaissance, and now as then the more temperate followers of the new way are seeking to reconcile its tendencies and methods with an orderly advance and improvement of existing institutions.

Imagination is essentially individualistic. Is it not also of the very essence of theoretical democracy? Of all forms of government, democracy is that form which abstains from laying the dead hand of one generation upon succeeding generations. Certain writers of late have represented the Constitution of the United States as a far more rigid and inelastic instrument than is commonly supposed. That it restrains amendment of its own provisions till there shall be time for second thoughts is unquestionably true and salutary. On the other hand, its provision for orderly amendment is one of its chief virtues and one in which it reflects the essential spirit of democracy. The Supreme Court, moreover, has inclined to

IMAGINATION AND MEMORY

the more liberal view, as is evidenced in opinions handed down within the present century. Mr. Joseph S. Auerbach of the University Council has called my attention particularly to the decision, delivered by Mr. Justice Holmes, in the case of Noble State Bank *vs.* Haskell,[2] to which Mr. Auerbach has referred in his *Essays and Miscellanies*.[3] This decision reads in part:

> It may be said in a general way that the police power extends to all the great public needs. It may be put forth in aid of what is sanctioned by usage, or held by the prevailing morality or strong and preponderant opinion to be greatly and immediately necessary to the public welfare. . . . If, then, the legislature of the state thinks that the public welfare requires the measure under consideration, analogy and principle are in favor of the power to enact it.

Apart from government, in the wider sweep of social relationships, the purely democratic spirit would set each oncoming generation free from the dead hand of the past, would set it free from dominating memories. In practice, this is impossible. A people who are attached to their own institutions and believe in them cannot be indifferent to the institutional allegiances of their children. That would not be human. Yet we in America have moved a long distance in this direction. It is doubtful whether in all history a generation of youth has been so left to the devices of its own imagination as is the generation now growing up.

6. We must now note the fact that such a course, in its extremes, means a deadening of imagination itself. Imagination run wild wears itself out. The reason of such futility is plain to see.

Imagination, even at its highest, cannot create from a void. It must build its castles from the materials of experience.

[2] 219 U. S. 104.
[3] Vol. 3, page 125.

A FEW REMARKS

What stark and inhuman construction may be expected from builders, however daring, whose conceptions have no enrichment from the history of mankind! I think we may see examples about us today. For the sake of imagination itself, the new generation requires a knowledge of the past. If it is to create a new world—new art, new religion, new governmental forms, a new morality—it cannot escape the world that is about it here, a world in which the comedies and tragedies of the past, its controversies, its philosophies, its poetry, have found their present-day embodiment. If the literature, the faiths, traditions, loyalties, of the fathers are not to be hammered into the memory and conscience of their children, the children ought at least to be exposed to an acquaintanceship with them, for in them is a wealth of sheer human life which they have kept alive while men have died. The younger race ought at least to have a chance of knowing the treasures of the generation from which they have sprung.

7. We may freely accept the fact that the mainspring of present-day education lies in imagination, a fact which marks this as one of the creative periods of educational history. For that very reason, this is a time when the responsibility of educational leadership is at its height. The free exercise of imagination being recognized as a crowning glory of this age, the age requires of its teachers the discipline of that imagination. I should venture to say that, in the broad and large, the educational problem of this time is the problem of the discipline of the imagination.

No doubt this use of terms is open to objection. Our psychologists can easily prove that there is no such *it* as imagination. They can go farther and prove, by experiment, that there is no such thing as discipline. I bow to their findings, though not accepting them as final, and continue to use these

IMAGINATION AND MEMORY

terms until a more precise nomenclature has been devised: *imagination* for that "leap of the spirit" which our civilization is taking under our very eyes, *discipline* for spur and bridle which may render that leap less perilous and more attaining; or, paraphrasing Tyndall, *imagination* for that power of expansion which is almost creation, *discipline* for that training by which it is to be chastened and controlled.

8. Imagination is to be disciplined by a persistent reference to realities, a persistent and understanding scrutiny of aims and methods. In the natural sciences, this is accomplished in part by the rigorous application of mathematics, in part by a highly developed practice of verification. In industry and business there is a practical discipline of results, which is decisive and sometimes appalling. In the great range of social and personal concerns—politics, morals, economics, religion—there is the rub, there is the supreme difficulty that education has to face.

In one way or another, the imagination of a new generation inevitably turns to the making of a new world. In different minds it sets off in different directions to devise a better life. The more it dominates any age, the more centrifugal and chaotic that age inevitably will be. Imagination is multiplicity incarnate. Its dominance in this age is one reason why the philosophic thought of the time so largely despairs of unity, finding its last word in variation. However, the natural craving for unity in the workings of the human intellect is not to be ignored. Moreover, imagination itself puts forth new unities, when the daring of a creative leader fires the spirit of many followers.

Every tenet in the dullest catechism that the youth of any age have had to memorize was in the beginning a fresh conception, an outreach, all aglow with prophetic imagination and kindling the spirits of many followers. But the attempt to discipline a living imagination by driving it back to predetermined unities of philosophic thought and social organization is not to be endured. A discipline of knowledge, however, is wholesome and necessary. To know the present world, it must be said again, is a condition necessary to the making of any new world that shall have in it the elements of stability and reality. And the knowledge of the present is part of it contemporary but a large part of it a knowledge of the past. Memory, after all, is an indispensable agent in the discipline of imagination.

9. It goes without saying that bare memories, indiscriminate and undigested, cannot render the discipline required. They are too prone to run into sheer prejudice and repetition. What we are coming to is this: that in those difficult fields of social and personal concerns, the task of higher education is that of creating the form of discipline vaguely known as criticism; and that criticism arises from a free interplay of memory and imagination.

The fact is often overlooked that in this group of subjects— the unsafe subjects, as some one has called them — we are dealing with one common form of experience. In all of them we begin with spontaneous preferences, likes and dislikes, loyalties and rebellions, and the task of the teacher is, not to drive these to predetermined conclusions, but to bring into them a finer and fairer discrimination—more intelligent and more coherent. Men of university training will never reach unanimity of opinion in these matters; but it is fair to expect of them a greater breadth of judgment, a greater wealth of comparisons, a more complete analysis of the problem in hand, than they themselves would have had without such training.

IMAGINATION AND MEMORY

Accordingly, a large part of the work of university teachers outside of the exact sciences is, whether implicitly or directly, the disciplining of students by way of criticism for their part in a world of projects and imaginings: not in order that they may be critical in the all-too-common sense of hypercritical, rather that they may better answer to the common wording of "constructive criticism," but still more that in habitual thought and conversation they may be resourceful in discriminating judgment.

10. It is in the fine arts and letters that criticism as the refinement of spontaneous preferences is chiefly recognized; but it is not to be forgotten that in politics and in all other social concerns in which personal choice—acceptance and rejection—play their part, we have to rely upon that intelligent discrimination which criticism connotes. The case of the fine arts is not unique. It is typical.

In no other of the arts can the working of a "chastened" imagination be so distinctly traced as is the case in architecture. In architecture, moreover, we have an obvious interlocking of art and industry, in which each has plainly influenced the other, while the architectural influence reaches far out into other domains of our common life. In no other field of artistic achievement has the creative imagination of American artists produced so deep an impression beyond our national borders. To catch some sense of what has been accomplished in this field we have only to recall a few of the names which mark our architectural advance within the past half century: Hunt, Jenney, Post, Richardson, Burnham, McKim, Root, White, Sullivan, Gilbert, Cobb, Cope, Hastings, Day, Cram, Howard, Bacon, Rogers, Howells, Goodhue, Delano, and how many others? The list might well include more names of those who are still in the full tide of

A FEW REMARKS

their creative activity.[4] All of those here mentioned, even the most insurgent among them, have responded to influences proceeding from the history of their art. Some of the most adventurous of them had undergone the rigorous, traditional training of the École des Beaux Arts. All of them, on the other hand, have shared the imaginative outreach of their time, and have gone out to match the spirit and the conditions of a new age with appropriate modes of construction and design. The relations of architect and client are often attended with difficulty, yet the very composing of their differences has its influence of an educational character. The professional educator, who sees his problem in the large, in its national and historic bearings, will find in the history of our American architecture an interpretation of his whole undertaking.

11. It is worthy of note that the imagination of the age is reflected in the higher ranges of American scholarship and teaching; and it is a cause for gratification that, in the best examples, when scholarship has taken wings it has still answered to the bridle of reality. We may take two books of the present century as pointing this moral, though in widely different ways; namely, Henry Adams's *Mont-Saint-Michel and Chartres*, and John Livingston Lowes's *The Road to Xanadu*.

In *Mont-Saint-Michel and Chartres* we have a titanic concentration and evaluation of mid-medieval history, as it found expression in one of the supreme examples of thirteenth-century architecture. As was inevitable, this adventure in

---

[4] I am indebted here to two recent books for the general reader; namely, Fiske Kimball's *American Architecture* and G. H. Edgell's *The American Architecture of Today*, as well as to numerous earlier works, and still more indebted to friends and acquaintances in the architectural profession, whose informal talk, at odd times over many years, I have found most stimulating and informing.

IMAGINATION AND MEMORY

scholarship fired with imagination has called forth the condescending comment of an occasional scholar in some special field, like that of Mr. G. C. Coulton in his *Art and the Reformation*.[5] On the other hand, we have the discriminating estimate of Mr. James Truslow Adams in the latest number of the *Yale Review*.[6]

> If the whole of the mediaeval story is not to be found in its pages, it nevertheless remains the best introduction for anyone who would reach to the soul of that period. As a synthesis of the thought and aspiration of one period in history, it would be difficult to find its equal. It has been of great and continued influence in America from the time when, against his wishes although with his consent, it was given to the public by the American Institute of Architects, which also elected Adams an honorary member.

The Road to Xanadu is in a double sense a revelation of the workings of imagination, first in the mind of a poet and secondly in the mind of a scientific-humanistic scholar. The book traces minutely the ways in which Coleridge amassed his particulars and fused them into two of the most imaginative poems in the English language. But in accomplishing this result, Professor Lowes has not proceeded as an encyclopedist, making an inventory of facts, but has made his readers partners in a scholarly excursion and has shared with them the road to each new discovery. To do this without compromising the scientific quality of his work is an achievement. His severest critic, Professor Lane Cooper of Cornell, credits him with "pursuing his quest tirelessly and independently, and doing more in it than all his predecessors combined."[7]

It would be too much to claim that a few publications such as these indicate a decisive trend in the productive scholarship

---

[5] Page 338.
[6] Vol. XIX, page 286.
[7] *Publications of the Modern Language Association of America*, Vol. 43, page 583.

A FEW REMARKS

of America, but it is a pleasure to record the appearance in this country of works of advanced and genuine scholarship which are so lighted up with scientific imagination.

12. The part which imagination has played and is now playing in religion, opens up a limitless field, in which education is intimately concerned—an alluring field, which I shall leave untouched save for a note in passing.

It is plain to see that the imagination of this age is turning with new zest to the problems of religion, but when has there ever been a time that human imagination was not playing—and agonizing — over these problems. Mysticism, heresies, conversion, crusades—next to human love the emotional life of the world has poured its main currents into these adventures. To capture the daring faith of one age and induce it to work in harness for the ages following has been the supreme occupation of the human intellect through all human history. The very difficulty of the task has been reflected in the hardness of the creeds, philosophies, moralities, and institutions in which it has found expression. In our own age, this embodiment of the memory of a great spiritual life is meeting with the freest speculation that the world at large has ever known, and the most recent science is quickening that speculation. Those great humanitarian visions that appeal most strongly to the spirit of youth, the amelioration of the conditions of labor, the improvement of the intercourse of races and of nations, are permeated throughout with religious aspiration. How can the higher education stand aside from this great stirring in the mind of our age? And where else can the discipline of a free imagination offer more exacting and absorbing opportunities to our educational leaders? The history of religion and the discriminating study of religion in its present-day relationships seem to me one of the finest and most

IMAGINATION AND MEMORY

necessary aspects of university education in this present generation.

13. Is the free range of imagination in present-day education to lapse into another age of dreary memorizing as has happened in the past? Examples of such flaming up of new hopes, followed by subsidence into pedagogic dust and ashes, might have been drawn from the ancient world as well as from the Italian Renaissance. Is history to repeat itself in this particular?

Who can tell? But it may be that some lasting gain has here been made. In one respect at least the teaching profession is on a different footing from that of any former age. By the establishment of teachers colleges and schools of education in our universities, a channel has been opened up through which whatever of spiritual life those institutions may at any time enjoy will find its way directly to the schools of the people. If science and scientific method shall keep imagination at high pitch in our higher institutions of learning, there can be no question that these newer departments, sharing vitally in the intellectual life about them, will go on vitalizing our schools of every grade.

IV

ON URBANITY

Introduction to the Annual Report for the Year ending June 30, 1927

IV

ON URBANITY

I WISH to discuss briefly some of the characteristics and responsibilities of an urban university, such as arise from the simple fact that it is urban, or are affected by urban conditions. The background of such a discussion is too obvious to dwell upon: the modern growth of cities, both absolutely and relatively; the inventions which have made such growth inevitable; the ways in which the city is projected into the country; the peculiar services which great cities render to the country at large; the world-family of cities and their sense of cousinship; their dominant virtues and their disheartening vices.

Out of this conglomerate of what everybody thinks and everybody knows, there emerges one personal experience of my own, repeated from day to day: the overpowering impression that this world-city of New York is changing beyond all past experience; that the forces which make for change are gaining here in momentum, like the gain in falling bodies; and that the part of a university in this environment is new every morning, fresh every evening, a field for the best wisdom that our age can command. What is true of New York in this regard is true in some measure of all the greater cities of America and of Europe. In this discussion, I am concerned with the general elements of the situation, not as we find it in New York alone, but as it appears everywhere in the cities of our modern world.

A FEW REMARKS

Its institutions of science and the arts are, no doubt, the crown of a city's life; but if they are to hold their preëminence they must gain in ennobling influence as the city gains in power. They must give increasing cause for civic pride where competing splendors claim the admiration of a growing body of citizens. They must mold the sciences which in their turn are remolding the city and the world at large.

1. Let us look for more specific connections, and first of all in the domain of public administration. The government of any one of our cities is today wrestling with difficulties—material and human—which arise from an accelerated growth. Here in New York the Mayor has appointed a City Committee on Plan and Survey, to advise upon some of the most pressing of these difficulties. It is not unlikely that a permanent bureau or commission on city planning may come from this temporary organization. Other cities have led New York in this manner of undertaking, notably Paris and Berlin abroad, and Chicago and Cleveland here at home. Back of these official undertakings, there is a long history of unofficial labors in this direction, in which within recent years the Russell Sage Foundation has had a part that is widely known and recognized.

But while planning for the future our cities are overwhelmed with immediate perplexities. Where scientific invention has had so large a part in their making, scientific research is increasingly required in the solution of their governmental problems. Such research ranges from the smallest details, respecting purchases, paving, fire protection, records, and other items innumerable, to the most fundamental questions in government, public law, economics, ethics, and æsthetics.

As a general rule, problems of detail may best be investigated by the agencies of practice, and problems of underlying principle may best be investigated by scientific agencies. In governmental affairs many researches must be carried on in the bureaus of administration, while those of a more fundamental character can best be prosecuted in universities. But on either side, success leads to expansion and overlapping, and the only boundaries to be drawn are those of the most effective operation. The more intimate the relations between the two groups the better.

What will bind them together most securely and most fruitfully is that all shall be dominated by scientific method and pervaded by the scientific spirit. With this end in view, it is desirable that the departments of a municipal government be closely related in their researches with the scientific departments of universities.

2. In the next place, let us make note of the relation of an urban university to the general system of education, public, parochial, and private. The reign of natural law comes every day more actively and consciously into the life of our citizens. While government prescribes, for example, certain sanitary observances, science goes farther and is gradually forming sanitary habits beyond the scope of governmental regulation. In countless directions, natural law is extending its jurisdiction. But it takes an intelligent people, intelligently instructed, to keep step with this advance. More than ever before, the teachers of the young require constant access to fountains of learning. Besides, the universities on their part profit by intercourse with the schools. Their physical sciences keep edging over into the biological sciences and the biological sciences keep edging over into the sciences of humanity, with the result that a university requires, for its full development, laboratories of society, observation stations of the social mind. Its working

theories in these higher fields of study cannot be adequately verified or corrected without reference to society as it is, including society in the making as it appears in schools for the young. In particular, its theories of education must take account of education in all of its stages, from the lowest to the highest, and must find grounds for the harmonizing of their diverse aims and processes. Under urban conditions, it is possible to render the interaction between the system of elementary and secondary schools on the one hand and the university on the other hand peculiarly intimate and unremitting.

3. Again, beyond the operation of government and popular education, we have to consider those private and semi-private agencies which are constantly at work for social betterment. They ramify in every direction and defy enumeration. Throughout this maze of experimental advancement, there is need of the closest connection with advancing knowledge as represented in the higher institutions of learning. The amount of wasted effort which is involved in these private undertakings for the public good is beyond calculation. Yet waste is better than stagnation, and to keep alive the effort toward improvement is clear gain, beyond the improvement which the effort attains. Such effort can best be kept alive where the steady inflow of scientific knowledge reduces the waste and increases the rate of efficiency and success. Moreover, universities on their part have need of daily contact with these expressions of human aspiration, as essential elements in the problem of human life.

4. We have next to consider the prodigious concentration of industry, commerce, and finance, which forms the material basis of a city's greatness. Knowledge has always been required in this field, theoretical knowledge beyond that handed down by tradition in the several occupations. But now we find

tradition revolutionized almost from day to day by new knowledge and new inventions. In so far as these new developments relate to practice and to detail, they can best be cared for in the occupations concerned, particularly in their several corporations and subsidiary agencies. But innovation is continually striking its roots deeper, into the very center of things, into our underlying conceptions of the world in which we live; and here, if nowhere else, it becomes a concern of the universities.

At this point, however, we encounter certain tendencies, relatively new, affecting the whole fabric of research, particularly in its relation to business affairs. We must turn aside for a brief review of this trend. It concerns certain aspects of coöperation.

5. The pith of what I have said hitherto is this: that urban conditions accentuate the interaction of our major human activities with the scientific pursuits of the universities; and that we must expect the several departments of government, education, commerce, industry, and agencies of social betterment to come into more direct and continuous connection with corresponding university departments. This may all of it be taken for granted, but the movement of the time is carrying us into a domain that is far less familiar and obvious. The lines of demarcation between the several sciences are wavering. The more important researches now spread over groups of two or three or many sciences.

The chief of the British meteorological service declared not long ago that further improvement in weather forecasting must wait upon more accurate knowlege of the physics of the atmosphere. That branch of knowledge, in its turn depends upon a whole group of related sciences. Meanwhile aeronautical development depends upon meteorology, and not only that, but upon a full range of other sciences, from mathematics to psychology.

Just now in the Boyce Thompson Institute for Plant Research, a strategic concentration of the sciences has been organized for the mastery of certain problems in the growth of plants most valuable for food. These problems could not be solved by any one of the sciences in an isolated laboratory. Attempts in that direction have magnified the truth of the saying, "divide and be conquered."

In further illustration, I may quote from Henry Fairfield Osborn's address on "Recent Discoveries relating to the Origin and Antiquity of Man," delivered before the American Philosophical Society in April of this year:

> In the great drama of the prehistory of man converge all the many branches of science which have been cultivated and encouraged by the American Philosophical Society since its foundation two hundred years ago. In fact, we do not progress very far in this most difficult, as well as most noble, branch of biological research if we pursue pathways which are purely anthropological or purely archæological. . . . Even Jupiter nods when the purely specialistic pathway is pursued. In the triumphs of modern astronomy, four sciences converge, . . . in the triumphs of anthropology, . . . no less than twelve of the major and minor branches of science converge.

Similar examples might be drawn in great numbers from the professions and other leading occupations, as well as from the domain of science in and of itself. They point to at least two conclusions of a practical character: first, that if science is to lend its full support to our enlarging practice of life, it must be, not alone or chiefly by way of single sciences, but by way of groups of sciences, working in unison; secondly, our universities, with their sharply departmental organization, are as yet inadequately prepared to meet the requirements of such coöperative research.

ON URBANITY

Under these circumstances, we are witnessing the development of independent laboratories and departments of research in a number of our leading industries. The fact that university laboratories are only partially equipped and that university professors have other demands upon them than those of research have undoubtedly a bearing upon the case; but I think one chief reason why so much of research, even that of a fundamental character, is breaking away from our universities, is the one which I have just now indicated. Laboratories of special research the industries must unquestionably have, but the farther down their researches go into underlying principles of science, the more they will inevitably turn for confirmation and interpretation to the institutions that represent the integration of all the sciences. Their own group researches will more and more tend in this direction. Meanwhile, the universities on their part must become more clearly representative of science in its integration as well as in its differentiations.

This conception of a university found a classic expression three quarters of a century ago, in John Henry Newman's *The Idea of a University:*

> I lay it down that all knowledge forms one whole . . . for the universe in its length and breadth is so intimately knit together that we cannot separate off portion from portion . . . except by a mental abstraction. . . . Sciences are the results of that mental abstraction. As they all belong to one and the same circle of objects, they are one and all connected together; as they are but aspects of things, they are severally incomplete in their relation to the things themselves, though complete in their own idea and for their own respective purposes; on both accounts they at once need and subserve each other.

This is not the place to consider those bearings of Cardinal Newman's doctrine with which he was himself preoccupied;

but his view of a university not only as a place where "any person can find instruction in any study," as Ezra Cornell proposed, but as a place where all subjects shall reinforce one another and unite in an unbroken circle and commonwealth of learning, is an historic conception which is receiving fresh confirmation in our time. Shall we expect our present-day universities to realize this conception? In so doing, shall we expect them to hold their own and play their part in an age which is producing independent and colossal agencies of research in special fields, industrial and professional?

The latest of our great industries to establish a general department of research and technology is the United States Steel Corporation. It has entered upon its new undertaking with a thoroughness that promises large results. At the annual meeting of the stockholders of the Corporation held in April of this year, Governor Miller, its general counsel, made the significant statement, "Your corporation has passed long since beyond the point of a mere private interest; your corporation has become in many senses quasi-public." Judge Gary, in announcing to the same meeting the establishment of the new department, reiterated this sentiment. "The whole public," he said, "is going to be immensely benefited by what we hope to produce in our laboratories, as the result of the studies our scientific men are making."

That part of the public which is centered in our universities is particularly interested in such an undertaking and will have a supreme concern in the reciprocal benefits that it foreshadows. It is hardly necessary to remind the group of scientists whom the Steel Corporation has called into its service, of the importance of continuing relationships between such a technical department and the scientific life of universities. Professors Johnston and Millikan and their associates, no less than Secretary Hoover, are well aware that the lasting vitality and fruitfulness of special researches, however scientific, depend upon their maintaining connection with science—that is, with science in its fundamental and comprehensive development; and that science, however pure, may hope for inestimable gains from the leadings of research in technical fields.

While the considerations here set forth are in no way peculiar to universities in an urban environment, they are magnified daily by the titanic forces at work in such environment, and are here thrust visibly upon the academic consciousness. An institution so placed and influenced should as time goes on acquire a certain leadership in the larger field of coöperative scientific undertakings.

6. I have deliberately approached my general topic from the side of research rather than from that of teaching, graduate or undergraduate. Now let us turn to a consideration of the graduate schools of these universities.

Historically, in this country, graduate schools are an afterthought and research is a by-product of the higher education. The afterthought and the by-product are now blended, although they are not by any means coterminous. I think we may anticipate some separate organization, within the universities, of such researches as are not concerned with the advancement of students to higher degrees, particularly researches involved in the coöperation of a university with the professions and industries. Even so, the two sides will have many points of connection. The younger researchers will generally serve their first apprenticeship in a graduate school, on the way to a higher degree. On the other hand, a professor whose primary concern is research will ordinarily draw to himself a group of assistants, among them candidates for degrees. It is probably fortunate that advanced teaching and pure research are generally intermingled, but care must be taken that neither one shall thwart the other.

There are particular influences which are contributing to the development of great schools of graduate studies in urban universities. One of these is the desire of junior teachers in neighboring schools and colleges to go forward under competent direction into the advancing lines of their several subjects and themselves to share in the exhilaration of that advance—a desire which is prodded, no doubt, by the professional advantages attached to the Ph.D. degree. Another is the belief that, particularly in economic, sociological, and educational fields, the concentrated humanity of a great city offers peculiar advantages for study.

It cannot be denied that some of these graduate schools have grown with perilous rapidity. The dangers lie in several directions. Productive scholars in our faculties have their scholarly product limited or at the worst completely checked by the necessities of graduate teaching. Even then, such teaching must in undue measure devolve upon the less mature members of the several departments. Moreover, classes quickly grow beyond the norm of most efficient teaching or leadership in research.

In the main this great demand for graduate teaching is to be welcomed and encouraged, but we can easily foresee the necessity of a rigorous limitation of the numbers of graduate students to be accepted by any one department or any one professor. Such limitation will vary according to the circumstances of particular cases. Financial considerations will render the need of such restriction more acute. Whatever may be said of undergraduate colleges, a graduate school cannot begin to be self-supporting if its classes are to be held to reasonable size and are to be supplied with adequate equipment for their

ON URBANITY

special studies. Our graduate schools must have generous endowments if they are to do the work that a scientific age requires of them.

7. When we come to the undergraduate departments of a university, the situation presents other aspects of unusual interest. As compared with the traditional American college, established at a distance from the greater centers of population and living as a world within itself, the collegiate departments of urban universities show advantages and disadvantages.

Colleges of the type (or types) represented, let us say, by Amherst, Vassar, Haverford, Knox, and Randolph-Macon, bring together students in great variety, from various environment; yet, from the point of view of the American people as a whole, their student body is comparatively homogeneous, drawn mainly from our older American stock, to be educated in its traditions. This is their strength and their weakness. The attendance upon the collegiate departments of our state universities, particularly in states having a large urban population, is more varied; while a university in one of our greater American centers of population, an "urban" university, will show the utmost diversity in its body of collegiate students, with a larger representation of the newer strains in our population than appears in institutions of the other types I have mentioned. This, again, is *their* strength and weakness, and it cuts out their collegiate work for them in an unmistakable way.

The danger that the newer America will overbalance the older America in these undergraduate departments is a real danger at the present time, but not necessarily a permanent danger. It is by no means true that the newer is crowding out the older altogether. On the contrary, large numbers of

A FEW REMARKS

the students of these institutions continue to come from the homes of Colonial Dames and Sons of the American Revolution. The country from one end to another is sending to the cities a rising stream of students who seek from preference, their own or that of their parents, the kind of education offered by an urban institution.

However, an exceptionally high percentage of the undergraduate body of an urban university will ordinarily come from homes in the city and return each night to those homes. They will miss the experience of transplanting for the term of their college course. Many of them, too, will come from homes without any tradition of higher education. They will themselves be pioneers in those higher fields, so far as their family associations are concerned—a fact of no little importance—but the family tradition will keep its daily hold upon them.

Daniel Defoe, writing early in the eighteenth century of the academies of the English dissenters, at one of which he had been educated, spoke of one of their greatest defects as a "want of conversation." In a different way this is what many of the students in an urban college miss. Accordingly, it is a lack which the authorities of urban institutions seek with especial solicitude to furnish. That students who do not reside at the university should have meeting places for collegiate intercourse is no small part of their concern, and that the wholesome incidental activities of college life, social, athletic, literary, shall have play, as circumstances may permit. The high cost of grounds and buildings in a great city stands constantly in the way of a full realization of these aims. The needful provision of dormitories, athletic fields, and the housing of non-athletic student activities goes forward in the face of difficulties, but it is still to be expected

ON URBANITY

that the collegiate education of students in an urban university will be predominantly scholastic and intellectual. To some of the critics of American education this condition would not seem wholly undesirable.

One favorable aspect of such a situation is suggested by a recent writer in *The Bookman:*

> The young man who labors assiduously today does not do it in some sequestered spot where he has no choice but to study; he does it in spite of the hullabaloo of modern society, and he achieves an able control of his mental processes by steeling himself against rivet machines and amiable acquaintances.

8. The immediate presence of noisy and remunerative employments has other consequences. Students who are "working their way" through college find in the city a great variety of opportunity for incidental earnings. Students who are making choice of their permanent occupation in life find the possible fitting and employment of their individual aptitudes spread out before them in bewildering variety. Within the university, the problem of bridging the historic gap between liberal and vocational studies opens up new lines of thought and invention. The interweaving of university training with the work-a-day life of a great people can here be carried forward under most favorable conditions, in close connection with that coöperation in research which has already been mentioned.

There is another aspect of the case that calls for notice. In the city, a university has all about it great numbers of mature men and women, employed by day in various occupations, who are hungering for education and more education. It is a hunger that is sharpened by the presence before their very eyes of college grounds and buildings, with abundant facilities for teaching. The drawing power of such a vision is great, and it is reinforced by the driving power of commerce and the industries, which are constantly increasing their demand for educated intelligence. The result is that the physical "plant" of universities in our cities has come to be used at night as well as by day, for the accommodation of these part-time students, and has thereby vastly increased the educational return from an investment in costly equipment.

Meanwhile, our conception of adult education has changed. Instead of an incident and a makeshift, it is now seen to be an essential and permanent aspect of modern society. In a world of accelerated change led on by scientific discovery, the man in mature life requires not only that his stock of information be brought down to date, but that his educational underpinning be overhauled from time to time, or at least be inspected and, if need be, reinforced. This is true of the "educated" as well as of the half-educated. According to the newer view, an educated man is one who is making good and continuous progress in his interminable education.

From the point where the high school finishes its work and on indefinitely, there is work for the agencies of higher education, not only with those who may still, for some years longer, give their whole time to an established curriculum, but also with those engaged in the practice of life, whatever their occupation and at whatever stage of educational advancement they may have entered upon it. In this an urban university has unbounded opportunity not only for an invaluable service to society but also for exploration in educational fields not yet mapped out nor crossed with well-worn trails.

9. I have stressed the scientific aspect of these institutions, though using the term science in its more comprehensive sense. When we turn to the fine arts and the newer humanities, we find that the educational importance of an urban center—and

ON URBANITY

particularly a metropolitan center—is magnified. That a university should conduct its teaching of these subjects in an environment enriched by great collections of sculpture and painting, by musical organizations of the first order, by the theater in a wide range of its activities, by the editorial offices of book and magazine publications and of metropolitan newspapers—it is a situation to quicken the imagination and stimulate endeavor. The innumerable coteries and the casual meetings in which art and letters are subjects of daily discussion by craftsmen, creators, and connoisseurs produce a current of ideas which even the roar of traffic cannot overwhelm. Without these refinements of the higher life, an aggregation of people, no matter how large, cannot claim the historic dignity of a "city."

In his essay on *The Literary Influence of Academies*, Matthew Arnold has a striking passage on urbanity, as over against provinciality:

> In the bulk of the intellectual work of a nation which has no center, no intellectual metropolis like an academy, . . . there is observable a *note of provinciality*. . . . The provincial spirit . . . exaggerates the value of its ideas for want of a high standard at hand by which to try them. . . . Not having the lucidity of a large and centrally placed intelligence, the provincial spirit has not its graciousness; it does not persuade, it makes war; it has not urbanity, the tone of the city, of the center, the tone which always aims at a spiritual and intellectual effect, and not excluding the use of banter, never disjoins banter itself from politeness, from felicity.

Mr. Arnold, to be sure, was discussing the tone of a city on the plane of its highest cultivation, and thereby laying himself open to no end of banter on the part of those who know the city—any city—on its lower levels. But to know a city in its refinement is unquestionably as important as to know it in its vulgarities. An urban university renders a significant service when it interprets the city, to the city itself and to a great body of students, in terms of its best.

How far a university shall directly promote or superintend constructive and creative work in literature and the fine arts, as in the useful arts, is not a question to be determined by drawing arbitrary lines. There are trivialities to be avoided. On the other hand the more recent studies in the workings of the human mind disclose so intimate connections between thought and action, between knowing and making, that we may view the extension of university teaching into any of the arts with more of hope than of apprehension. A case in point is the service that Professor George P. Baker has rendered the American stage, first from his "workshop" at Harvard and now on the fine foundation which Mr. Harkness has provided for him at Yale. But in any case we may say here, as was said of scientific research, that the more fundamental inquiries, at the least, are certainly appropriate to the character of a university.

This, I take it, is preëminently true of criticism. It hardly need be said that the word *criticism* is used here in its larger sense, as a discriminating search for the better and the best. Such criticism involves a knowledge of the history of the art concerned and of related arts, and of the long thought of mankind on art and life, back into the ancient classics and out into the wider range of philosophy. It requires a grounding in university studies.

It would be hard to exaggerate the importance of constructive and convincing criticism in the life of a great city. Here we see lavish expenditures on entertainment and adornment. Criticism is to enable a people to discipline and refine their own instinctive preferences in these directions and to turn their expenditures, of their own better choice, into ways that will yield the more enduring satisfactions. Such a people will

ON URBANITY

encourage our artists to their best endeavors. Criticism moreover will render our artists themselves more clearly aware of their own ideals and more exacting as regards their own performance.

So we must regard the work of an urban university in the fields of music, letters, and the arts of design, as an integral part of the making of a modern city—which is always in the making; while from the other side we shall regard these humanities in their urban development as necessary to the best development of the university. We may expect every one of the arts to have connection in various forms with its related department or group of departments in the academic organization. Mere locality is not enough. There must be active intercourse if such proximity is to eventuate in reciprocal benefits.

10. There are other interests in life, of capital importance, into which the instinctive preferences of men enter largely, with the same need that taste and choice therein be disciplined by knowledge. Politics is one of these. What has an urban university to do with politics?

The university is indebted to the city in tangible ways—for police and fire protection, with freedom from taxation, and in many related particulars. It is affected by changes affecting the honesty and efficiency of the city government. The members of the university are members of the community in which they live. They have their individual obligations, but for the moment we may pass these by, and give attention instead to the corporate obligations of the institution, as a center of teaching and research.

It is plainly inappropriate that the university should enter into details of partisan controversy. It is equally plain that back of those controversies and running through them are

A FEW REMARKS

questions of historic truth and philosophic principle with which universities must concern themselves. Are universities limited here to empty generalities? We must admit that a just delimitation of their sphere of political influence is difficult. That is a problem which has come down through the centuries, and is not to be settled today by any simple formula. Certain considerations may be mentioned, however; obvious all of them, but maybe not too obvious:

A university department of politics or government — or sociology or economics—should be a center of accurate information regarding the government of the city in which it has its being and of other cities, and of the best thought of the world upon municipal affairs. It would be an anomaly if such a department should be better equipped for a study of the politics of ancient Rome than for a study of the politics of the home town. Nevertheless, the politics of ancient Rome, and of modern Rome, for that matter, should not be left out of its comprehensive view.

There may undoubtedly be occasions in which local wrongs of so flagrant and fundamental a character become the center of partisan conflict, that a university would be justified in throwing the weight of whatever influence it may have on the side which stands for the correction of those wrongs. Even then it would not be justified in acting upon the sudden impulse arising from a sharp political campaign, without dispassionate consideration of the question in its multitudinous relationships.

Nevertheless, a university has some underlying responsibility for the betterment of the life around it. If American cities continue to be known as the worst governed in the world, the universities within their borders will bear some measure of that burden of reproach. They must labor incessantly for the

ON URBANITY

recognition of sound principles of political activity and political integrity, even while they are aware that in practical politics those principles will be variously and discordantly interpreted, even by their own members and graduates. In any case, it may reasonably be expected that their graduates will go out into the larger life of the community with some kindling of civic imagination, some affirmative conception of the greatness to which the city may aspire when it shall be governed with intelligence, good taste, and righteousness.

11. There are other aspects of urban life and of the relation of universities thereto which invite attention: the learned professions, labor and its manifold problems, recreation, the church and religion. But I must not prolong this discussion. A few words should, however, be added respecting the general tone of city life, using the word in a somewhat broader sense than Mr. Arnold had in mind.

Where a vast population is crowded thickly together, its group-consciousness may be intensified and at times a mob-psychology may be developed. But this is not the chief result. Instead, in our cities we see lesser groups developing intensely within the all-embracing group. Because of the crowd, these draw their skirts more closely about them and defend themselves by alliance with those of their own kind. All manner of exclusiveness is cultivated. Under these conditions, the typical service of universities is peculiarly desirable. It is their province to cultivate learning in disregard of the influences which keep men apart from one another. They increase the chance that intellect and character of whatever origin shall make its way and win its own associations, friendships, and rewards. They lessen the chance that the crowd, as one unthinking mass, shall be swept by sudden passion into dangerous excesses.

A FEW REMARKS

This is a task for university men and women in our cities, wherever their individual course of education may have been pursued. It is peculiarly a task for those who have been bred in institutions within bounds of the city itself, and it is to the interest of the city that its home institutions shall be maintained on such a level of excellence and influence as shall enable them to play their full part in this work of civilization.

Especial emphasis must here be laid on the part of universities in exalting the intangible values of life. Americans are charged with inordinate devotion to the American dollar. The charge is not wholly justified, but it has its measure of truth. Our men of greatest wealth are not, generally speaking, the greatest sinners in this respect. Some of them are among our militant idealists. It is not wealth that is making for materialism but the exaggerated pursuit of wealth, not money but the love and worship of money. There are undoubtedly great areas of life where this low cult predominates to the practical exclusion of all other thought or conversation. To spread abroad an efficient idealism among those obsessed with this mass-psychology, passionate and unlovely, is a task which centers in the cities of our land. The means to the end are not weapons of direct attack but the slow germinal infiltration of ideas. It is the part of universities to deal with ideas as things with inevitable growth in them and to plant them unceasingly in the commercial and industrial life of the community. When we realize that our national spirit is changing from the predominant rural-mindedness or village-mindedness of a generation ago to a predominant urban-mindedness such as is now beginning to appear, we get some intimation of the significance of the part to be played by urban universities in fostering the higher life of our American cities.

These paragraphs are intended not as argument but as exposition. I have not sought to claim superiority for universities set in an urban environment, nor to admit inferiority, but rather to suggest what the city may mean for the university and what the university may mean for the city. No university can be a merely local institution. If it is a university it is of the universe. But locality has a bearing on the fortunes of any institution, and ought to have. And where the factor of environment is chiefly human, overwhelmingly human, its significance in this interplay of influence is important. It is of equal concern to our universities and to the nation that the institutions of science and the arts shall not be overshadowed in the amazing growth of these great centers of population but shall continue to be the crown of their life.

I have made no attempt here to define an urban university. Some of these institutions are privately managed and supported, as is the case with New York University; others of them are created and maintained by the state or by the municipality. Some that were originally established in the country are now in the way of being enveloped by a neighboring city. Many a college town today is fast growing into a city. If the views herein expressed are true, they may be found to have a bearing upon the life of many institutions which are not consciously or conspicuously "urban."

I may take my final word from the program of the Société des amis de l'Université de Paris, as set forth in the latest issue of the *Annales* of that Society:

Il n'est aucun de nos concitoyens qui ne profite chaque jour, directement ou indirectement, des travaux accomplis dans les bibliothèques et les laboratoires de l'Université de Paris. Il n'est aucun de nos concitoyens qui ne puisse, en échange, s'intéresser à ces travaux en s'inscrivant parmi les "Amis" de cette Université.

A FEW REMARKS

The universities that are steadfastly making their way in our American cities cannot match the dignities which that lofty Mother of Universities has gathered unto herself with the ripened learning of her centuries. But they join with her in the endeavor to make the cities of this modern world the honorable debtors of their institutions of learning, down even to the humblest of their citizens.

V

BEAUTY AND THE UNIVERSITY

Introduction to the Annual Report for the Year ending June 30, 1932

V

BEAUTY AND THE UNIVERSITY

MANY years ago, David Swing, a leader in the earlier intellectual life of Chicago, delivered a stimulating lecture on the historic progress of mankind from the beautiful to the useful. I have not been able to find a copy of this lecture, but its substance has remained with me. Of late it has set me thinking that, with the rhythmic tides in human affairs, beauty as a prime concern of life is sure to come back and play again a leading part.

Even now we may see the return wave setting in. Beauty cannot for long be regarded as incidental to more serious concerns. It is bread of our life. "Songs are as useful as plows." Moreover—and that is my excuse for any discussion of this subject in this place—as we become more conscious of this power permeating all human life as with the influences of the Pleiades, we have a growing sense of its importance in our education. Taking the sayings of David Swing as a point of departure rather than as a text, I wish to discuss briefly some question concerning the related elements of beauty and truth in our educational procedure.

1. The mere statement of such a question plunges us into a whirlpool of controversy—a thousand controversies rather than one. The literature of these conflicting opinions is appalling in its mass and variety; while out of the turmoil, *alto prospiciens,* emerge some of the most serene and inspiring works in our educational history. For the few comments I

wish to make, I shall have to pick my way cautiously among objections and contradictions.

We are told to begin with that the subject proposed can offer no question at all, since universities have always concerned themselves with both truth and beauty. Or, going more deeply, we are told that the two are one, as John Keats assured us, and that's the end on't. Or, Pilate's question is turned into "What is beauty?" and we are told that the modern world does not know and cannot decide what beauty is or what is beautiful, so why concern ourselves with conundrums? Or, more dogmatically, some writers in widening the meaning of art would narrow the meaning of beauty, running the Cinderella picture backward on the screen.

2. But let us dip into some familiar history. Students of literary origins, while differing heatedly upon particular interpretations, seem agreed in their emphasis upon the part played by music and the choral dance. If we except the codes of the lawgivers, the earliest literary expression was rhythmic in its character, poetry rather than prose. It was the elements of beauty in it that gave it its early currency and its continuing life all down the ages. That same carrying power within it made it the available material for civic and religious education, the only education sought in earlier times beyond apprenticeship in the ordinary doings of life.

How the earlier Greeks expanded the conception of music in education to cover the offerings of all the muses is a well-known story. Our Professor Tanner has brought to my attention a volume in which that story is told with extraordinary freshness and wealth of illustration. It is Kenneth J. Freeman's *Schools of Hellas*. The story of the book itself has a personal interest. The author had been the holder of undergraduate scholarships at Cambridge University, and in the

BEAUTY AND THE UNIVERSITY

year following his graduation became a candidate for a fellowship in Trinity College. This volume was prepared in satisfaction of the requirement that candidates for the fellowship present evidence of their scholastic competence in the form of a substantial piece of original work. The work which young Mr. Freeman presented was thoroughly original in that it went back rigorously to primary sources of information; it was permeated with the author's interest in education, which he had chosen as his own life-work; it is alive with human insight and interpretation; and it is crowned with a lasting pathos through the death of this young scholar three months before the election to the coveted fellowship was to take place and before he could give the final touches to his work. Even as it stands, the volume bears witness to the scholarly standards of Cambridge as well as to the individual scholarship of its young author.

The story of old Greek education is really necessary to any historical perspective in our study of modern education, but that story is not so simple a sequence as textbook accounts would lead us to believe. It is rich in variety and change. We can only note here, however, four trends of its later development, which had their influence in still later times; namely, the advance of sheer intellectual curiosity; the growing attention to language, with a view to precision in its use; the rise of philosophical systems; and the cultivation of oratory, both for persuasion and for disputation. It is easy to see how these trends are interrelated. Their impact upon Roman education, culminating in Quintilian, is another familiar story.

When Greco-Roman culture passed over into Christianity and Christianity penetrated the new peoples of the Western world, it was the intellectual rather than the aesthetic aspects of that culture which became dominant. The "trivium"—

grammar, dialectic, rhetoric—was the introduction to all formal education. Dialectic, with endless disputation, widened out into medieval philosophy, of which Aristotle was overlord and theology the crown. The organized universities, which emerged from this intellectual turmoil in the eleventh and twelfth centuries, were institutions for the ascertainment, the defense, and the propagation of truth. Beauty was ignored, or more likely feared and repressed as an enticement of Satan.

3. Meanwhile beauty, in poetry, architecture, music, was making ways of its own, of wonderful vitality, but apart from the universities. Even in the universities the poetry of Greece and Rome was not altogether unknown. But the preoccupation of the universities with truth in its severest intellectual acceptance, propositional and syllogistic, gave abundant occasion for the gibes and complaints of humanist teachers, when the Renaissance appeared upon the scene.

The humanists of the fourteenth and fifteenth centuries declaimed against the traditional education as regards both form and substance. For the Latin of the schools, barbarous as they delighted to call it, they would substitute the pure Latinity of the Golden Age. For the scholastic dialectic, with its disputations in philosophy and theology, they would substitute the Roman poets and writers of classical prose, with Greek added as Greek came to be more widely known. The mastery of truth and victory over error should give place to the ennobling influence of a majestic literature. The schools were to be pointed towards an aesthetic and humane rather than a theological ideal.

The successive stages of early humanism were broadly characterized by Mark Pattison in his volume on *Isaac Casaubon 1559–1614*. Of the earliest of these he said: "The classical conception of beauty of form reëntered the circle of ideas

BEAUTY AND THE UNIVERSITY

... after nearly a thousand years of oblivion and abeyance.
... The first period of the Renaissance passed in adoration of the awakened beauty, and in efforts to copy and multiply it."

4. This account must ignore no end of cross-currents, compromises, and hopelessly confusing tendencies of that period, in order to get at the fact with which this discussion is concerned: that the educational revolution accomplished (in part) by the Renaissance was essentially a turning from an ideal of truth to an ideal of beauty.

Let us recognize, however, the incompleteness of the mode of education traditionally directed to either the one or the other of these ends. Scholasticism, in its passionate devotion to truth, largely ignored the truth of the material world. The "quadrivium," to be sure, was supposed to offer concrete knowledge, but its four branches, geometry, arithmetic, astronomy, music, could have had in them but little more than a foreshadowing of modern science. The humanists, in their turn, were so absorbed in the cultivation of the ancient literatures that they could give little attention to the great developments in the creative arts which were going on about them, such as would have commanded the lively interest of the ancient Greeks. So a partial cultivation of the domain of truth, side by side with a partial cultivation of the domain of aesthetic taste, was characteristic of the earlier centuries of modern university education. (The "music" included in the quadrivium, with its lingering Pythagorean implications, could have had but little in common with the music of these later centuries.)

5. The history of universities in the centuries following the Renaissance — dreary enough in many ways — shows a varied blending of scholasticism and humanism. Grammar, which had served as the vestibule to dialectic, now served,

with but little improvement, as vestibule to the classical authors. It continued to darken the lives of schoolboys for many generations, a *janua* which for them was hardly ajar. The earlier humanism cooled its first enthusiasms in a hard and dry grammatical training, leading to rhetorical studies in which the Ciceronian tradition was dominant. The deeper insights of aesthetic criticism had hardly been approached.

For the nobler spirits of the time there was throughout a high devotion to learning, now in the form of classical erudition, now in that of the philosophical and theological disciplines. There were mighty controversies, in which faculties and individual doctors, champions of truth, were found now on one side now on the other of momentous questions. The divided Christendom of the Western world, European and later American, displayed on both sides that fine historic paradox in which the approach to all higher Christian teaching was made through a pagan literature. So we come down to the nineteenth century and to times of which men now living have vivid recollections.

6. Let us turn aside here for a glance at a comparatively recent book; namely, *The Aims of Education*, by Professor A. N. Whitehead. The author of this compact volume is too well known in academic circles to require more than a passing identification: the Cambridge and London University scholar who came to our American Cambridge some eight years ago as professor of philosophy in Harvard University. I have found the second and third chapters of this book particularly suggestive. They are entitled, respectively, "The Rhythm of Education" and "The Rhythmic Claims of Freedom and Discipline." The interesting point here is, not only that Professor Whitehead brings forward anew the idea of rhythm as related to the educational process, but that in doing so he

brings forward, in fresh associations, a conception which runs all through the logic of Hegel. That Teuton philosopher who so dominated the world of German thought in the second quarter of the nineteenth century was later thrust ruthlessly from his high estate, so that down to the present day the very word Hegelian is commonly used as a term of reproach. No one would look now for a reënthronement of Hegel in the realm of philosophic speculation. Nevertheless, there's a mighty music in his philosophy, to echo down the ages. We cannot forget its influence in American thought in the last quarter of the nineteenth century, through a notable group led by Dr. William T. Harris, with such independent leaders as Professors George H. Howison and George S. Morris at other centers. However, the mere fact that fruitful ideas from his system have been reappearing of late more frequently than twenty years ago can hardly be taken as a revival of "Hegelianism."

"I think that Hegel was right," says Professor Whitehead, "when he analyzed progress into three stages, which he called, Thesis, Antithesis, and Synthesis. . . . In relation to intellectual progress I would term them, the stage of romance, the stage of precision, and the stage of generalization." Professor Whitehead's discussion of these several stages, as they appear and reappear in the process of education, cannot detain us here, but it will repay any reader of those chapters that I have mentioned.

7. The next decisive swing of the pendulum came with the great development of the physical sciences, from the middle of the nineteenth century on, bringing with it laboratory methods of teaching and research, and a new conception of scientific truth.

It is easy to recall the tone of the physical sciences in the later years of the nineteenth century and the earlier years of the twentieth. It was confidently prophesied—by the minor prophets, chiefly—that science would shortly master the outlying provinces of human life and would become all and in all. We were fast approaching the full and acknowledged supremacy of physical law and a universal blue-print civilization. It is well to recall also the unfailing modesty of more thoughtful scientists, even in those days of triumph, a modesty which has become more generally characteristic of modern science, as it has pushed farther and farther along the borders of the unseen universe. We may well pay tribute at the same time to the tenacity and devotion of those humanist educators who held through all those years to an ideal of literary and classical culture, with its historic stress upon aesthetic values. It seemed a losing cause, but it had faithful adherents.

8. On the whole, the inductive sciences have dominated our conception of higher education in the twentieth century. In a different setting and with a different instrumentation, the function of a modern university has been accepted as identical with that of a medieval university; namely, the ascertainment, the defense, and the propagation of truth. But truth is regarded not as a static entity but as an attainment continually changing in that it is continually advancing. Accordingly, the emphasis has been shifted from defense to ascertainment, that is, to scientific research.

The chief reasons for this dominance of a science of observation and experiment are two; namely, the fact that its conclusions are open to objective verification or refutation by any competent scientist, and, secondly, that its results are readily available for the purposes of material invention. The consideration of human use is influential, but the chief

BEAUTY AND THE UNIVERSITY

consideration in the university world is that of truth. The vision of a body of apparently incontrovertible truth, constantly growing by vital processes from within, and spreading throughout the range of human experience, and that with an inherent beauty of its own, is one that has given an intrinsic authority to higher education in our time. It has endowed our modern universities with an extraordinary influence in the affairs of mankind.

9. But this scientific age is witnessing developments of another kind. Humanity, human nature, is pushing forward into creative activities which science cannot anticipate. Self-expression, in individuals and in nations, lays hold upon the sciences, with their growing knowledge of the world that is, to make therewith a world that never was. It refuses to be cramped and confined by natural law, as natural law is thus far formulated. It is often impatient of both civil and moral law. Its impatience, in the newer generation, has been intensified by knowledge of what was accomplished through science in the World War, for the destruction of men and of civilization. But such impatience is more than mere reaction to the horrors and futilities of war. It is a product of modern democracy, but again, it is more than that. It is one of those tides in the spirit of mankind which may be creative or destructive in the ultimate effect. It is a composite of many impulses and many ideals, but in one way or another those ideals make their appeal in great part through a sense of what is aesthetically desirable.

10. In view of this great and multifarious upheaval, should we not look for a renaissance of beauty in our whole system of education? We may reasonably expect that such a revival will be wider in its reach than that of the fourteenth and fifteenth centuries. It will gather into itself knowledge

of the several arts, with creative effort and appreciation, such as lay outside the ken of those earlier universities, even after humanism had wrought its greatest reforms. Music, modern eloquence and poetry, sculpture and painting, and all-embracing architecture, will make their several contributions. It need hardly be said that this is not all of the future tense. The new renaissance is already on the way, has long been on the way, and has been only partially obscured by the glories of modern science. It is represented in our university history by a notable group of teachers of the past generation, Gildersleeve, Norton, Winchester, Stanley, Gummere, Barrett Wendell, Gayley, Woodberry, Fred Newton Scott, to say nothing of others of their kind, including those still in active service. These men and others, by sheer personal power and learning, held their own with the great teachers of the sciences who were reshaping educational ideals in their generation.

11. There are obvious weaknesses to be reckoned with when we consider university teaching on the aesthetic side. Beauty as a pedagogic aim, it must be admitted, has a deadly tendency to degenerate into prettiness and sentimentality. How can vigorous young minds, fresh from the exacting requirements of physical laboratories, be made to realize that art and letters are concerned with high realities of human life? They find their snap courses on the side of the humanities. Here the rigorous technique of instruction in the sciences is hard to match, and when the serious attempt is made, a poor imitation of scientific procedure is likely to result. The problem is one with which teachers of our time must grapple. Are they to find methods in their subjects which shall command respect and confidence from the side of the sciences, and at the same time shall not weaken but rather vitalize the character-

BEAUTY AND THE UNIVERSITY

istic appeal of their subjects? How shall they lend vitality to ideals and appreciations? This problem seems to me one of the most penetrating with which educational thought and practice will have to do in the coming generation. There are certain of its aspects to which I wish to call particular attention.

12. In the first place, the violent shiftings of taste in this generation are disconcerting. They seem due to two principal causes: the endeavor to reveal the unsuspected dignities and beauties of common things and even of things repulsive and hateful; and the respect paid to the revelation of unusual artist personalities, finding their own forms of self-expression, regardless of any canons of taste. Yet both of these causes are related to the rising power and responsibility of art in this generation and need not be unduly disturbing. Nor need we be shocked by the current dicta that art is not concerned with representation and that art is not concerned with beauty. They are an added accent to the demand that our teachers in the arts create more adequate systems of teaching in their field, and that they consider what is really their field and to what fields it is neighbor.[1]

In the second place, we have to reckon with the fact that the point of departure in all education of taste is the personality of the learner. In the natural sciences we must rigorously exclude the personal element, save as it must be calculated as a disturbing variable in our observations. In aesthetics, on the other hand, the personal element is the very material with which we have to do. Spontaneous, and often deeply prejudiced, opinions of approval and disapproval, are to be made over into deliberate and well-grounded choices. Capri-

---

[1] Professor A. Philip McMahon's recent book on *The Meaning of Art* gives a discriminating survey and appraisal of conflicting views. A suggestive article on "New Tastes in Old Prints" by William M. Ivins, Jr., in the September *Bulletin* of the Metropolitan Museum may be mentioned here.

cious aims and raw design in constructive activities are to be made subject to maturer purposes. His deeper aspirations are often to be discovered to the learner himself. We can arrive at any consistent elevation of taste and accomplishment only by way of an enlargement of the range of judgment, through acquaintance with unforgettable examples, and the play of thought on experience, individual and historical. We may call such method criticism, but the term is rather unfitted for such use by unfortunate connotations.

In the third place, we shall find this procedure widening out unbelievably. I have called attention elsewhere to the fact that it is essentially the same as that which must be followed in all the sciences of personal and social life. Sociology, politics, economics, psychology, education itself — these are half-sciences, in that they deal only in part with fixed laws and predictable reactions, and must give thought in no small part to the bent and genius of living men. What we have been considering in the serene atmosphere of aesthetics is found making its way into the very toil and turbulence of common experience, into the stern choices and ultimate decisions of life. Let the ratio of ascertained fact and governing principle in these sciences of human life rise without any determinable limit. There will still open out upon them that undiscovered country, in which lies all our hope for a better world, in this generation as in those to come. It will still be true as Robert Bridges has written in *The Testament of Beauty*, that

> Wisdom lies
> in masterful administration of the unforeseen.

What young graduates shall bring away with them from college will still find its farthest reach in that which goes out beyond their knowledge of nature and its laws, beyond their expectation of what science shall have in store for them in the future. It will appear, for some of its best, in a finer insight into the minds and purposes of men, and in a disciplined imagination, revealing to them the part that they may severally have in shaping the new days that are to come.

So in looking for a betterment in the methods and management of teaching in the field of beauty, we are in fact engaged in a wider search for improvement in all of those branches of instruction which look directly upon human attitudes and purposes, on the peculiarly human side of history in the making. If this conception is not amiss, then the responsibility for university education on the side of beauty, and its great brood of human values, is one of the weightiest with which we are concerned. It must go deeper as time goes on, deeper perhaps than we can now anticipate.

13. Both science and the humanities reach up inevitably into the domain of morals. It would be an arbitrary limitation or sheer abstraction if they were to be excluded from this domain. It is here that some of the sharpest differences between science and the arts appear. It is here, too, that the overlapping of their jurisdiction becomes most obvious, with both conflict and collaboration resulting.

When the science of the later nineteenth century was fairly entering upon its day of triumph, Goldwin Smith contributed to *Popular Science Monthly* a sane discussion of the question "Has science yet found a new basis for morality?" He referred with caution to theories then current—and still current —which would make of the human being an "automatic man"; and to the theories of Darwin, from which, as he said, inferences were drawn "which the discoverer himself has not drawn." He declined "to pronounce that the religious sentiment in man is devoid of meaning, and that the evidences are absolutely incapable of rational reconstruction." But on behalf of science he declared "no sane being doubts that the tendency of truth of every kind is moral, or that the tendency of falsehood of every kind, if persisted in, is immoral." A like pronouncement comes from scientists of the present day, with more of surmise regarding the new deeps that their science looks out upon.

It would be impossible to estimate the moral significance of the sense of truth and devotion to truth which are characteristic of modern science. As this spirit comes abroad in our age, issuing forth from innumerable laboratories, it takes its place as one of the chief stabilizing influences in a tumultuous world. It cannot remain the cherished possession of a class, a guild of scientists. Some apprehension of its authority has spread throughout all lands, and those are backward peoples indeed who have not felt its influence. Our universities would be untrue to themselves if they permitted any other consideration to dull the edge of this fidelity to truth as modern science has taught it. To that end they must foster scientific studies, in and of themselves, without subservience to ulterior purposes, without subservience even to moral purposes.

Now, while society is finding moral leadership in the natural sciences, within the realm of truth, it is likewise seeking leadership in other realms, beyond the realm of established truth. Truth is fundamental. The truth of physical science is priceless. Truth is not all. An age which gives rein to social imagination, marked by a rising sense of beauty, is now laying a great responsibility for moral leadership upon the arts, upon the humanities. There is even a disposition to make theirs the chief responsibility, on the easy assumption that religious sanctions have lost their power, and good taste must function in their place. Gilbert Murray remarked in

BEAUTY AND THE UNIVERSITY

one of his lectures on "The Classical Tradition in Poetry," "I confess I have never been able to see, though people have tried to point it out to me for forty years, any real difference between the moral and the aesthetic."

Herein we find an extreme attribution of power and responsibility to that side of life in which beauty is regnant. The subject is so vast and the literature of the subject is coming in such an avalanche, that I must here limit myself to the fewest words of comment.

In an age of shifting standards, we welcome every ally in the war against evil, which knows no discharge, and in the reinforcement of the good life, personal and social. Science is a powerful ally. Aesthetics, apart from extravagant claims and with less of obvious power, goes farther in the realm of spiritual insight. It shapes ideals and aspirations.

To give free scope to this power, beauty must be cultivated in our universities with as much seriousness as truth. That it may do its rightful work in the world, it must, like science, be cultivated in and of itself, without subservience to ulterior purposes, without subservience even to moral purposes.

14. It will be found, nevertheless, that science, art, and morals cannot be grown in separate compartments. The beauty that runs through science is not an unimportant aspect of science. Great scientists are found to be devotees of the arts, particularly of music, but beyond those individual manifestations, their science in and of itself reveals to them vistas of the purest beauty. Miss Millay's lines will be recalled:

> Euclid alone
> Has looked on beauty bare. Fortunate they
> Who, though once only and then but far away,
> Have heard her massive sandal set on stone.

A FEW REMARKS

On the other hand, in this age as never before, the results of science are material for art; while now as all the way down from the beginning the intuitions of beauty find their way to truth, outstripping logic and research. "The rest may reason and welcome: 'tis we musicians know."

Morals are bound up with both inseparably. The conditions of public morals are subject to all manner of scientific investigation; and art at its highest deals with human life as shot through and through with moral struggle, hope, and retribution, with love and death.

15. After we have brought science and aesthetics into better balance in our scheme of education, we shall find them supplementing each other and making for better citizenship in a better society. But we cannot escape the need that their convergence to such ends shall depend upon a discipline higher than either, and capable of determining their coördination. A university that is less than a school of philosophy is less than a university. It is only through syntheses higher than either physical science or the arts of beauty can of themselves accomplish that the continuing adjustment of higher education to the requirements of our social order can be consummated. It is not to be forgotten, moreover, that for many of the highest minds, in these days as in other days, such philosophy will eventuate in conceptions worthy of the historic appellation of theology, by whatsoever name they may be called.

Meanwhile, the philosophy which is to make any institution worthy to be called a university, however high that philosophy may aspire, will be indebted—and it may well be equally indebted—to the arts which make for beauty and the science which makes for truth.

And the useful? It will undoubtedly keep up its onward march, with the onward march of physical science. So should

BEAUTY AND THE UNIVERSITY

it be. But Heaven help us, in this generation, to set truth and beauty marching on ahead. They should direct its course to more complete and satisfying use.

VI

HUMANISTIC STUDIES—A FORECAST

From an Address delivered at the Celebration of the One Hundredth Anniversary of the General Theological Seminary, April 30, 1919

VI

HUMANISTIC STUDIES—A FORECAST

WASHINGTON IRVING, a hundred years ago, was issuing the successive numbers of the *Sketch Book*—the *Knickerbocker History* had appeared before that time—and we find him writing this to Henry Brevoort:

> All my ideas of home and settled life center in New York. . . . There is a charm about that little spot of earth, that beautiful city and its environs, that has a perfect spell over my imagination.

Meeting today in this mightier New York, with which these two neighboring institutions have grown to their present estate, we find ourselves in a world in which democracy is facing its supreme struggle hitherto. Democracy has triumphed over autocratic aristocracy only to plunge into a momentous conflict with autocratic anarchy. The nomenclature is chaotic but not more so than the situation. Democracy has come to be the middle ground. It now represents our main hope for stabilized social relationships.

This main ground of our hope, on the human side—what does it mean for our institutions of religion and education? Let me touch on two or three outstanding features of the case. You will surely forgive me if this presentation shall be fragmentary. Even on occasions of the greatest dignity and distinction, I have never yet known an assembly to show disapproval when a speaker has sacrificed logical continuity and completeness in the interest of brevity.

A FEW REMARKS

The first essential of democracy is that men, however differently circumstanced, shall understand one another and shall care to understand one another. This is so obvious a fact that it is often overlooked. It seems to call for reiteration. Is not this essentially a Christian attitude? Whoever has this spirit has in him, I think, some of the real stuff of Christianity. Yet it will take all of the Christianity there is at large to bring the Christian world into this spirit.

In the second place, the spread of democracy means coöperation. This again is so elementary a fact that its significance is disregarded. It means that the helpfulness of man to man is to be reciprocal. It rules out servility and it rules out condescension. The lion is to help the mouse in the same spirit that the mouse shall help the lion. And each is to feel the same sort of gratitude toward the other.

In the third place, leadership in our democracy is singularly inwrought with the daily life of the people. It is harder than ever for one set apart, whatever his throne may be, to give direction to a people's life. This fact has led some theorists to maintain that mass-movements of popular opinion will put an end to all individual leadership. This conception has profound religious implications—that the moving of the great waters is to make the ocean-stream of history, flowing resistless through its appointed course, flowing unchanged by what any man or institution can do to hurry or to retard or to change its ways. The raw stuff of a world-religion is here. But closer examination reveals the movement of the crowd as made up of the endless interaction of manifold forms and grades of leadership. The greater and the lesser prophets are still there, and their word is precious, down to the least of them, whenever they speak truth.

In the fourth place, the higher life of our democracy cannot be considered as apart from our economic life. In every form of human society from the beginning this has been measurably true. But history, under the spell of ethics and aesthetics, has walked backward with averted gaze, to hide the shame. Our democracy, on the other hand, is finding new dignity, of humanity and service, in the daily need and the daily toil; is finding there a more rugged aesthetics and ethics. How shall people live their life in that part of life in which they are making a living? This is a concern of our newer democracy, an open and an honorable concern.

To what end do these considerations lead, as regards our coming education? They would seem to indicate, clearly enough, that the education that is to be will be predominantly humanistic. The obvious emphasis as we emerge from the war is on the side of the physical sciences. I cannot believe that this is to be the decisive and lasting emphasis. The deeper concern that we have brought with us from out the shadow of the conflict, is the concern for humanity, the gnawing hunger in our souls for a betterment of all human life.

The student body in our colleges has been gravitating, since the armistice was signed, toward chemistry and the several branches of engineering, with some indications of a similar drift toward medicine. These tendencies are natural and are not to be deplored. There is plainly a great work to be done by engineers, by chemists and physicians; and students are going forward to meet the age of reconstruction in making their preparation for these scientific pursuits. But as we study the trend of the time it becomes manifest that a returning current is to be anticipated, a second phase, perhaps, of the new education movement, which will concern itself more immediately with those human needs that loom large through the dimness of our day. More and more the engineer finds that his problem of construction is conditioned by the spirit of the men who are to do the work. The physician finds that he cannot rest with the treatment of his individual patients, but is carried forward into problems of community sanitation which are part and parcel with the social problems of the community.

Here is, indeed, a distressing paradox: at the same time that the demands for technical knowledge are advancing, the man who is merely a technical expert finds himself more and more in the position of an employe. His services are bought and paid for by men of larger vision. His captain and employer deals with the most intricate and exacting operations, not as interests beginning and ending in themselves, but as related to the wider needs of human society.

It is plain that the elements with which we are here concerned are not the same as those that have borne the name of humanism in the past. One is tempted to speculate with reference to the particular branches of study that may forge to the front in the tumult of these times. At one time you will say that psychology is slowly making its way to the leading place, a discipline which has the advantage of being both scientific and personal. At another time, economics, particularly in its more human aspects, seems to be a very "man-of-the-hour" among our studies, the one that is to command the greatest following, if not numerically at least as regards its attendant throng of ideas. Perhaps the science of sociology might mediate between these two and become our very science of sciences. No one can say with any certainty. But each of these sciences is changing, to become less deductive and analytic; each of them is enlarging to take into its view the atmospheric qualities of humanity. Their scope is widening, too, to embrace a psychology of nations — a psychology, a social science, of mankind. And every day makes more evi-

HUMANISTIC STUDIES—A FORECAST

dent the fact that to be a full-grown citizen, or a master of any industry, of any business or profession, one must have somewhat of that organized knowledge of the human race.

I must resist a temptation to speak of other departments of knowledge as related to our new problem of studies. But before I close, I should like to say a few words regarding the place of history in our new curriculum—or let us say, of historical studies, since we must realize that history is broken up already into many lines of instruction and research.

You will recall that passage in Sismondi's *History of the Italian Republics* beginning with the words, "History has no true importance save as it teaches a moral lesson. It should be explored, not for scenes of carnage, but for instruction in the government of mankind." More and more is it clear that the moral teachings of history, its instruction in the art of government, are not specific lessons. For history has been made in the past and will be made in the future altogether by the doing of unprecedented things. History is a record of surprises, of departures from the beaten track. The greatest master of historic science cannot predict what may happen tomorrow in Paris or in Rome, or furnish government with formulæ to meet the crises of the new-born day.

The service of history goes deeper. It ripens our short-lived experience, with the sun of other years and other generations. It stabilizes our judgments, the judgments of our narrow time and place, by wider comparisons, reaching out into all the ages. It gives us a profounder knowledge of humankind. In so doing, it guards us against a reckless spirit of iconoclasm.

Yet it would be a mistake to regard history simply as a bulwark of conservatism. A renaissance has commonly begun with the reëxamination of a traditional civilization. It is a

A FEW REMARKS

fresh start from the beginning of things. In like manner, every new generation must find itself and form itself through a reinterpretation of its heroic traditions. The severer methods of historic research in our day and the rediscovery from time to time of documentary evidence, renders history in the modern sense a sword of power, a very maker of new history.

The record of recent centuries must obviously be rewritten in the searching lights cast backward from this War. And that rewritten history will have incalculable influence in the molding of our new democracy.

For you whose faith, in the stricter sense, is represented by this Seminary with its hundred years, and by many institutions with their many hundreds of years; and for all of us whose lives have been shaped and nurtured by an historic Christianity: the future of research and teaching in the field of history must be of capital importance. It goes without saying that such research and teaching must be free. The corollary of that freedom must be found in ripened knowledge and a matured sense of high responsibility.

The faith we cherish, the faith we would spread abroad, is faith in the eternal verities. We know that what is new has a moving appeal for unstable natures, in a time of sweeping change. We know, moreover, that what is new and only new shall in its time grow old—that the only things that never grow old are the things that never were new. We know that childish natures, and stronger natures, too, grown tired at last with disappointing novelties, will come drifting back again, a-hungered for the things that shall endure. What overshadowing responsibility must, then, be theirs who in each new generation shall seek to separate the truth that is eternal from those accidents, attendant circumstances, which cling to it as if they would deceive the very elect.

HUMANISTIC STUDIES—A FORECAST

No small part of this responsibility, in the years immediately before us, will fall upon our students and teachers of history; of institutional history, of the history of culture and the history of thought, and of the mighty literatures of our historic civilization. Any forecast then of new developments in our education must give an important place to the historical sciences and disciplines, and the teachers of history and its related subjects must bear their part in the making of the age that is to be.

VII

SOCIETY AND SOLITUDE

Opening Address of the College Year, delivered at University Heights, September 30, 1925

VII

SOCIETY AND SOLITUDE

SOME of you are familiar with Emerson's essay on *Society and Solitude*. I shall not imitate Emerson today, nor compete with him; but I am going to speak on the same subject, *Society and Solitude*, though from the point of view of college life.

What has brought this subject into prominence just at the present time, is the issuance from the Press of the University of Illinois of a remarkable volume, a translation into English of Petarch's *Life of Solitude*. A notable publication, simply as a piece of book-making. But see what it is as a contribution to pure scholarship. Here is a long essay, written in the Ciceronian Latin of the fourteenth century by the foremost litterateur of that age, which first appeared in print a century or so after it was written, and now appears for the first time in an English translation. The work of the translator, Professor Zeitlin, is not pedantic, but it bears the marks of competent scholarship. He has made available for English readers another monument of that great period in the history of European civilization.

I am not recommending this particular book for your reading. It is good reading; nevertheless there are others, better known, which are more to the purpose of the general student. But I should like in passing to say a word of generality regarding the use of great books of other ages in a course of education. One or another of these books will give pleasure, and set for you a new standard of taste. That is worth while, but it is not enough. You need a wider and more varied reading in these fields in order to help you meet one of the most modern and most insistent needs of practical life, the need of an understanding of men.

You can know men jauntily and plausibly without such aid. A genius may know men more deeply by a kind of divination, uncanny and incommunicable. But I doubt whether any man can know his fellow man truly, both his *esse* and his *posse*, save as he discovers him through a knowledge of mankind. How can you sense his quality and motives, unless you know something of those enduring qualities and motives which have lived through the life of the ages? How can you appraise them, without knowing the higher levels which humanity has from time to time achieved? A generous acquaintance with the historic master-works of human art and thinking, a wide and appreciative acquaintance with them, is the natural means to this end; and that is what is known as a liberal education.

So of this or any other work of a great era or a great master, one may say, "Here is another trail, into unknown areas of the human spirit." Every great book, when you look into it—a new book or an old—finds another Balboa there on his mountain top.

But the elder Mr. Weller might say, "I am afeerd that werges on the poetical." Let us come back then to my topic:

You will hear much said about society. You will be told that association with other men is the main thing in your college life, that to play your part with men is the main outcome of college life. That is true, all of it true. I have paid my respects to this doctrine in what I have just said about a liberal education. But now the thought is of solitude. It is the thought that you are to have within you a refuge, where you can be alone, even while you mix with the crowd; and that you shall put that retreat to worthy use, which the crowd can neither give nor take away.

I can illustrate by an ancient tale and by a modern history. The tale is that of a hunter who went gunning for wild fowl. He came to a pond which was fairly covered with wild duck. He fired right into the flock and they rose in the air and sailed away, all of them sailed away. He was amazed. The flock was so dense that he could not have missed them all. He followed after them over the brow of the hill. Then he saw that ducks were dropping to the ground, dead ducks and lame ducks, any number of ducks. The explanation dawned upon him. They had been so crowded together that when the flock rose in the air, it carried all of the birds along with it, alive or dead. This is a fable for the lame and for the dead, but chiefly a fable for the living, whose life is in themselves and not altogether in the gang.

The modern history, is from Burton Hendrick's *Life of Walter Page*. "Page," he says, "had a characteristic way of thinking out his problems. He performed his routine work at the Chancery in the daytime, but his really serious thinking he did in his own room at night. . . . He would enter the house slowly . . . go up to his room and cross to the fireplace, so apparently wrapped up in his own thoughts that he hardly greeted members of his own family. A wood fire was kept burning for him, winter and summer alike; Page would put on his dressing gown, drop into a friendly chair, and sit there, doing nothing, reading nothing, saying nothing—only thinking. Sometimes he would stay for an hour; not infrequently he would remain till two, three, or four o'clock in the morning; occasions were not unknown when his almost motionless figure would be in this same place at daybreak. He never slept through these nights, and he never even dozed; he was wide awake, and his mind was silently working upon the particular problem that was uppermost in his thoughts. He never rose until he had solved it or at least until he had decided upon a course of action. He would then get up abruptly, go to bed, and sleep like a child." Some of you will recall the tension caused by the sailing of the steamer *Dacia* in 1915, and the surprising but perfectly simple way in which this case was handled by our Ambassador. Mr. Hendrick goes on to say, "Page discovered this solution on one of these all-night self-communings. It was almost two o'clock in the morning that he rose, said to himself, 'I've got it!' and then went contentedly to bed."

I shall not point the moral of these examples. You have all of you passed our intelligence tests. But what a college we should have, what classes, what athletics, what fraternities, dramatics, journalism; what a country we should have, what industry, what institutions, politics, and social life; *if:* if every man among us brought into his corporate and coöperative life some fruit of the spirit, serenely ripened in the walled garden of his inner life; his secret dealings with truth and ambition and beauty; his reading of books and his thought of what he has read; the amusement and the inspiration he may find in afterthoughts of his intercourse with men; the inner resource, the waters drawn from springs of unselfish affection; the cheerful dance with daffodils, which enables him to wait for trains at a dismal station without unbearable boredom, or to endure, with vibrating attention, the boredom which others may have thrust upon him.

It is in the life of the religious recluse that the cultivation of solitude reaches its highest pitch of intensity—its best and its worst. I have no thought of prompting a college student to

SOCIETY AND SOLITUDE

be a recluse of any kind. But I say nevertheless that the best and ablest among you will develop the power of withdrawal from the world, on occasion, for the freshening of your lives. The best and ablest have always shown the ability to protect themselves

> From fools who crowded youth, nor let thee feel alone.

The philosophical thinker must do his severest thinking alone. The master of scientific research must have this power. Their absorption lies close to religion. They have use for the times of wakefulness at night. The words of an ancient singer come home to such as these with peculiar force:

> When I remember Thee upon my couch,
> And meditate on Thee in the night-watches. . . .
> I remember the days of old;
> I meditate on all Thy doing;
> I muse on the work of Thy hands. . . .
> What is man, that Thou art mindful of him?
> And the son of man, that Thou thinkest of him?
> Yet Thou hast made him but little lower than the angels,
> And hast crowned him with glory and honour. . . .
> In the night I will call to remembrance my song;
> I will commune with mine own heart.

But they who commune with their own heart, if only they go far enough to find their ultimate self, chastened by silence, its clamorous ego sifted out and cast aside—they cannot but touch the hem of religion in that experience; they will find that to be alone is to have other companionship. Though it be but for an hour or for a moment, if it be sincere and unequivocal, their feet will have rested upon another world, and have caught from it new vigor, such as Antæus never knew.

These are the thoughts that I wish to leave with you at the opening of this new year. It is hinted to me that some small

A FEW REMARKS

minority among you will find that I am talking "over your heads"; not as regards intellectual ability, oh no, but as regards intellectual interest. If it be so, I am glad. For my own part, I tire of what is too familiar, too obvious, too comprehensible. I crave that which requires at least some moderate exercise of thought to follow it through. If any of you have, even a little, stretched your comfortable intellects to grasp an unfamiliar subject this morning, I am glad and rejoice with you. To others among you, these words of mine are as a familiar song, so often you have traversed this ground before, either in your own cogitations or in the pages of some familiar and favorite author. You I welcome to a fellowship in the pursuit of ideas which, however simple in their beginnings, may lead you far; for here our way runs side by side with some of the main highways over which the generations of thinking men have traveled down the ages.

There are many things to be said to you at such a time as this in the way of homely and expected advice regarding the conduct of life in college. But, in so far as they do not go without saying, you have been told these things already and will be told, by your deans and faculty advisers, to say nothing of the picturesque and penetrating admonitions which you will receive from your fellow students in classes more advanced than your own. There are lessons, moreover, which are irresistibly driven home in our military discipline, and others equally forceful which are learned only in those strenuous labors which go by the name of "sport." I need not cheer you with pages of advice. I need not tell you to wear your overshoes when it rains, for on every side they will warn you not to let your feet grow cold.

Nevertheless, in all seriousness, let me remind you that the supreme association of college life is that of students with teachers. Within their limits, the University authorities have spared neither care nor cost in the assembling of learned men, with skill to teach, for the making of your college faculties. It is your privilege to know these men and to be their fellow-students. Many of you, I have no doubt, will find your solitary hours enriched to the end of your lives with memories of this priceless intercourse. Many of you will say of this one and that one of your college teachers that, save for the intimacies of your own homes, to have known that man as teacher and friend was the highest privilege that life has given you.

Finally, let me come back to that volume of the great Florentine, with which I began.

"Each man," says Petrarch, "must seriously take into account the disposition with which nature has endowed him. . . . For there are some for whom the life of solitude is more grievous than death . . . and this will happen particularly with persons who have no acquaintance with literature. Such men, if they have no one to talk to, are destitute of any resource for communion with themselves or with books, and necessarily remain dumb. And indeed isolation without literature is exile, prison, and torture; supply literature, and it becomes your country, freedom, and delight. . . . Besides, I never persuaded those for whom I said solitude was advantageous that in their desire for solitude they should despise the laws of friendship. I bade them fly from crowds and not from friends. And if any one thinks that he possesses crowds of friends, let him first see to it that he is not deluded. . . . There is the joy of having elevated thoughts, and conversing with comrades of the spirit, and beatific visions, and of oft commanding the presence of Christ in intimate communion . . . and so the human spirit . . . from a guest and stranger becomes a member of God's household. . . . I am not, however, so unrea-

A FEW REMARKS

sonable in my attitude or so narrowly attached to my view as to think all others foolish or to compel them to pledge fealty to my doctrine. Many may be brought to profess, but no one can be forced to believe. There is nothing more vital than independence of judgment; as I claim it for myself I would not deny it to others. . . . Let provision first be made that, after the prosperous conclusion of his mental toil, one may be enabled to put off the burden of his weariness by having easy access to woods and fields. I deem that those who ponder philosophy, and even more those who brood on poetry . . . must be left to their own devices. . . . They raise themselves aloft on the wings of their genius, for they must needs be carried away with more than human rapture if they would speak with more than human power. This, I have observed, is without doubt achieved most effectively and happily in free and open places. Wherefore I have often looked upon a mountain song as if it were a frolicking goat, the gayest and choicest in the whole flock, and being reminded of its origin by its native grace, I have said to myself,

Thou hast tasted the grass of the Alps, thou comest from above."

VIII

SCIENTIST AND ARTIST

An Address delivered before the Academy of Medicine of Northern New Jersey, March 16, 1927. Reprinted from the Journal *of the Medical Society of New Jersey, 1927.*

VIII

SCIENTIST AND ARTIST

WE all know that increasingly we are living under the reign of natural science. Physicians, of all men in the community, are aware of this fact. The scientist is king. He is in the saddle. But what I wish to point out tonight is that he does not ride alone. The artist continues to ride with him. You will recall the saying of Dogberry's, "An two men ride of a horse, one must ride behind." Now as regards the scientist and the artist it depends upon circumstances which is to ride behind. It is sometimes the one of them and sometimes the other. And now and then there is the inevitable scramble to see which one shall ride in front.

What I mean by *scientist* is what is generally meant. But the sense in which I am using the word *artist* may not be equally clear. We commonly think of an artist as one concerned in the making of beauty. Musicians and painters, at one end of the scale, and sartorial and culinary artists at the other, have all of them this characteristic in common, that they are all concerned with matters of taste. But I am giving the word a still wider meaning tonight. If a scientist is one who learns and knows, an artist is one who makes and does. For the present, let us disregard the limitations of taste and beauty, and extend the term to apply to the production of things useful as well; or let us go farther yet, and say that while the scientist is one who seeks to know the world as it is, the artist is one who seeks to make it different.

A FEW REMARKS

The achievement of useful results, when it rises above mere tradition and artizanship, is commonly referred to as applied science. Here is the domain of the professional practitioner, of the engineer, the modern banker, the surgeon and physician: artists all in the larger sense; masters of applied science. But note this fact: no one of these arts and professions is the application of a single science. A profession is not the mere servant of any one of the sciences. It has aims of its own, methods of its own, territories of its own. Within its range, it is itself king, and the sciences are there to serve its purpose.

Consider this profession of medicine, on which our interest centers tonight. So far as that group of sciences is concerned which has to do with our bodily health, the physician calls upon them one and all according to his need. He organizes their findings in his treatment of a given case. When he reaches their present limitations, he must still go on, as it were in the dark, summoning his own experience and creative imagination and that of his professional predecessors and associates to do what he believes to be the best for his patient, walking by his matured professional faith and not by sight.

He calls to the sciences, "You have given me the mastery of diphtheria, of tuberculosis, of yellow fever; now give me the mastery of pneumonia and of cancer." And the sciences may well reply, "We have not given you the mastery of any disease. We have given you materials of knowledge which you have organized into a victory of your own. We shall continue to give you these materials of knowledge as fast as our researches can bring them forth. But it is the art of your profession which must make them serve the purposes of healing. We are to make discoveries, sometimes at deadly cost. You are to invent the ways in which they are to serve a human need, and your invention, too, may be achieved at deadly cost. Each

SCIENTIST AND ARTIST

must have his part, and neither scientist nor artist will have done his perfect work till each has entered into the labors of the other."

It would be well for us all if the artist might know something of science, not in its uses only, but in and of itself; if he might know the detachment and exaltation of one who seeks truth not for its applications but for itself alone. And well, too, if the scientist might know the devotion of the artist, who considers what his work shall mean for the good of mankind. It would be well if each might share somewhat in the essential life of the other.

Now and then in the history of the world there appears a man who is scientist and artist both, and that in well-nigh balanced combination. The supreme historic example of this union was Leonardo da Vinci. The wealth of the spirit which found embodiment in this great figure of the Italian Renaissance, has come only recently, within this present generation, to the general knowledge of mankind. Born in the territory subject to Florence, forty years before the discovery of America, the natural son of a young Florentine notary, acknowledged and educated with the greatest care by his father, he manifested a capacity and passion for both science and the arts that are the wonder of modern scholars who have explored the records of his career.

What field of knowledge and activity did he leave untouched? For centuries he has been known as a consummate painter. He was no less a sculptor and an architect. But he was also an engineer, a musician, a geographer, a physicist. On the new building of the Daniel Guggenheim School of Aëronautics at New York University are inscribed four names of those who have contributed most to the conquest of the air. The first of these names is that of Leonardo. He could not be content to represent the flight of birds, till he had inquired into the mechanism and method of their flight. He could not be content to paint a landscape, till he had gone deep into the principles of perspective and the laws of sight, the effect of atmospheric conditions, the botany of trees and flowers. His sculpture and portraiture rested upon a comprehensive knowledge of human anatomy, acquired through a more patient and intelligent dissection than the whole history of medicine had produced before his time. A century before Francis Bacon, he conceived the method of determining physical laws from phenomena, observed and experimental. Yet when he undertook to paint, he was altogether the creative artist, using his scientific acquirements according to his need, not as the servant of knowledge but as its master: alive to the deeper mysteries of the human spirit and ensnaring them upon the canvas, as in his *Mona Lisa;* alive to the deeper aspirations of religion in an age of harsh religious controversy, and bringing them to light in the majestic sweetness and sorrow of his *Last Supper*.

You may think my comparison far-fetched and fanciful if you will, when I take this master-artist of the fifteenth century as representative or symbol of the medical profession of the twentieth century. His art rested upon the scientific study of anatomy, as does yours. But that is a superficial resemblance. He was an artist, who made the sciences tributary to his art— any science that would serve his purpose. The art that was then at its height was painting, and in this art his greatest triumphs were achieved. The art of healing was still in the depths. Today the two arts of medicine and engineering are in the ascendency. In one of these the medical profession achieves its immediate triumphs; while in sanitation, medicine and engineering join their endeavors, to accomplish untold good for the human race. Let Leonardo, the artist of beauty four centuries ago, stand as representative in some sense of these arts of human use in the twentieth century.

Why must we believe there is an impassable gulf between the arts of beauty and the arts of use? In this age of the world, an impassable gulf is a gulf to be passed. Beauty will not stay put. In so far as it is the real thing, it breaks away, like Pegasus out of his stall, and wanders over the earth. It finds its affinity and reflection in the most unlikely places. Is there any art that has more to do with ugliness and nastiness than has the art of the physician or the surgeon? But it is all the while doing a work of redemption. Beauty for ashes. Lilies, white and gold, made from the mud.

A beautiful thing is health. When a surgeon performs a clean and perfect operation or a physician, after accurate diagnosis, applies the effective remedy, how can you keep esthetics out of his contemplation of the result? No, I did not say *anesthetics;* but I realize that I must enunciate carefully, or these walls, from long custom, will give back the sound of a medical term. I said *esthetics*—the sense or science of beauty. A reckless columnist has said that a thing of beauty is a boy forever. When one of you has saved the life of a boy and sent him on his way to vigorous manhood — or a girl either, *mutatis mutandis*—you would not deny that among the satisfactions of that accomplishment is the sense of something beautiful that has entered into it. And when you have made a beautiful old age possible to any individual, who without your skill would have gone down into a miserable existence or an early death, you may well look upon your work with an artist's appreciation and see that it is good.

But enough of that. Let us turn to another point of view, namely, the coöperative aspect of your profession. As human undertakings increase in magnitude, it becomes more and more necessary that men should work together for community ends, conceived and sought in common. Examples lie all about us. The larger purposes involve greater foresight. So the medical profession is now concerned not only with the treatment of individual cases affected by particular diseases, but with the treatment of disease in its wider scope, as affecting whole communities or the whole human race, and with treatment taking the form of prevention as well as of cure. You are familiar with these facts, and examples in great number will occur to you: hookworm, tuberculosis, yellow fever, malaria. Just now the profession is entering upon a study of common colds, which so greatly reduce the economic productiveness of our people. The cure of a patient is still the immediate concern, but the complete eradication of a disease, the world over, is now an ultimate aim.

What a tremendous development of human coöperation the pursuit of such an aim involves! Laboratories, engineering, insurance, organization for health and sanitation, municipal, state, national, and international, private and governmental. The scale of such undertakings is awe-inspiring and their ramifications are bewildering. And we must go a step farther yet. Your profession may not stop with the prevention and eradication of disease; it will doubtless go beyond, into the problem of establishing the physical soundness and efficiency of the nation as a whole. Here it comes, more distinctly than ever, into relations with the ethical and spiritual forces of our people. For physical soundness and moral sanity cannot be divorced, when you are dealing with the people of a nation or the race of men. Without physical soundness grounded in moral sanity, a people or a race cannot permanently endure. In the course of centuries, they will fade away from the earth, in spite of all the physical antiseptics and prophylactics your profession or any other can provide. So your profession, more and more, finds itself under the necessity of coöperation with other professions, with education, religion, all of them in fact, for the accomplishment of the ends of human life upon this earth.

In this conception, too, there is beauty, is there not? But beauty on so vast a scale that it may rather be described as grandeur, majesty, sublimity.

If you seek a conspicuous example of the larger service of the medical profession—and there are many of them—you cannot do better than turn to the career of William Crawford Gorgas. To have cleared Havana of yellow fever, to have done a like service at Panama and rendered possible the completion of the great canal, to have achieved the incredible results recorded in the general health of the American Expeditionary Force in the World War—this would seem to be more than enough for the life-work of any one man. Yet in his perfect modesty, General Gorgas refused to taken even the credit that was due him, and brought to the front those who had worked under him, and particularly those who in other professions, civil and military, and in scientific research, had worked with him, to make possible these marvelous results.

From this wider survey, let us return to the simple relationships of your art to the progress of the sciences.

At every step, you make new applications of science; you make new demands upon the scientist. As rapidly as possible, you replace tradition and intuition with ascertained and systematic knowledge. In so doing, you not only increase the percentage of your successes; you do two things besides, which are a gain to mankind. In the first place, you put the sciences to a test beyond the testing of the laboratory; you discover gaps and flaws in what the scientist has taught; you lead him on to fresh inquiries. In the second place, you educate the community. You teach your patients and their circle of acquaintance to have faith in the findings of science. You teach them to live under the reign of natural law. That is great gain, when science still must make its way against a tide of misconception, ignorance, and prejudice. You may go farther, and educate your clientele to take the teachings of science with discrimination: to take them gratefully, but with a grain of salt. For science, too, is incomplete, and some of its confident utterances of today will be modified tomorrow.

The very fact that science is advancing and therefore changing, accentuates the rôle of the physician as an artist. He must choose from available knowledge what will apply to the case in hand. In the face of conflicting hypotheses, he must give due weight to experience, insight, common gumption, common sense. He must have the humility that will learn from the successes and failures of others, even from those who are not of his school. He must take account of heredity in his patients, of personal idiosyncrasies, of home surroundings. In all of this, he is an artist; and if he shall bring true scientific knowledge into working agreement with true intuition, he shall be recognized as a genius of his art, a priceless possession of the community and the nation.

It is with a rank outsider's view of your task and your achievements that I pay tribute tonight to your profession. It is a profession to which I and my house are immeasurably indebted. I think of those physicians who have helped us in times of physical distress and mortal danger, and I am grateful beyond measure for both their science and their art. Most of all, I am grateful for their humanity. These are feelings which I cannot adequately express, unless it be in the words

SCIENTIST AND ARTIST

of an ancient writer, who wrote for all peoples and for all the centuries. I turn to the sayings of Ecclesiasticus:

"Honour the physician for the need thou hast of him: for the most High hath created him. For all healing is from God, and he shall receive gifts of the King. The skill of the physician shall lift up his head, and in the sight of great men he shall be praised. The most High hath created medicines out of the earth, and . . . hath given knowledge to men, that he may be honoured in his wonders. By these he shall cure and shall allay their pains, and of these the apothecary shall make sweet confections, and shall make up ointments of health, and of his works there shall be no end. For the peace of God is over all the face of the earth."[1]

[1] *Ecclesiasticus*, XXXVIII, 1–8.

IX

ONE AND ALL

*From the Baccalaureate Address delivered at
University Heights, June 3, 1928*

IX

ONE AND ALL

A UNIVERSITY education, as I see it, in all of its schools and departments, converges upon the teaching that the good of One is to be gained through the good of All. That is the substance of what I shall have to say today.

There may be some absolute individualists in the world—a hermit, perhaps, or a miser—but they are negligible. Almost every man that you meet lives a part of his life in the life of others. Even the supreme egotist takes other men into the sanctuary of his private ambition. They give him applause. They are necessary to his life. The educated and the ignorant alike find a part of their good in the good of those about them. That is of the very nature of mankind.

Some do this narrowly and passionately; some widely, superficially, negligently. But to do it intelligently, that is another matter. Here education has a part to play, and the higher you go in the scale of education, the more impressive and inspiring is its part in this moral expansion of life. Let us see how this works out in the various departments of university study.

Take first the humanities. There is the field in which to improve one's practice of discrimination, as between the better and the worse in the products of the human spirit. There is the field of criticism, if you mean by criticism the raising of our instinctive likes and dislikes into reasoned preferences, rich in comparisons. If this is to take the form of a mere fastidious aloofness, its value to society may be questioned. But that is not the form that it takes where college teaching is at its best. Terence may not have meant all that we read into his *homo sum*, but the better teaching of the humanities embodies the spirit that regards nothing human as altogether foreign.

In literature and the arts, two tendencies are characteristic of this present age, the search for beauty in things commonplace or ugly, and the expectation of beauty in any spontaneous expression of human nature. Both of these tendencies have led to ridiculous excesses, which the slow verdict of the years will reject. But both of them are enlarging our sense of essential brotherhood; they are widening the roof under which we gather those whom we recognize as our own. An education in the humanities which did not sharpen the student's sense of difference would be only a near-education at best. But where the sharpening of that sense means a keener apprehension of essential values, whatever their setting and surroundings, it is a thing to be prized; it confers a new capacity to find the good of one in the good of all.

Take then the study of the natural sciences. Here we are concerned with the mastery of natural law, impersonal law. What has this to do with our sense of personal good, our own good or that of other men? The sciences undoubtedly lead to inventions, and so give us more effective instruments for making our way in life, but what have they to do with making life better, with ennobling its relationships?

I think they have a part in those moral relationships which is often overlooked. Impersonality is a step to a finer personality, even as skepticism may be a step to a higher faith. Let us dwell for a moment on this view.

In our egotism, particularly in the sensitive egotism of

adolescence, we need a powerful wrench to set us free from the morbid self-reference which dominates our life. The egotism of later years is deadlier yet, forever asking the brutal question, "What is there in it for me?" This same sordid questioning may creep into the study of the sciences. That must be admitted. But not into the scientific study of the sciences. To catch the true scientific spirit even for a little while, to accomplish the detachment of mind which pursues a natural law solely to learn what it is and how it operates, to put aside preference and bias, to give our inborn craving for knowledge a chance to assert itself against all baser self-expression and acquisition—that is to clear the way for a finer personality. That is to throw into clearer perspective our relations with our fellow men. And that is one great function of the sciences in our higher education.

The earliest of the sciences was astronomy. Before scientific method was known in its modern forms, a few choice spirits forgot their meaner selves in gazing upon the starry heavens. Astrologers sought to turn such observation to personal uses in ways that were often sordid and grotesque; but some there were all down through the ages, who having looked upon the stars turned back to their daily round of life with spirits purified and chastened, better fitted to see themselves and their neighbors in due proportion one to another.

You recall the saying of Immanuel Kant that, "Two things fill the mind with ever increasing admiration and awe the oftener and the more steadily we reflect on them: the starry heavens above and the moral law within." And that of the Hebrew psalmist: "When I consider thy heavens, the work of thy fingers, the moon and the stars, which thou hast ordained; what is man that thou art mindful of him?"

The studies of the modern laboratory may do for many a

A FEW REMARKS

student what communion with the starry heavens has done for a chosen few through all the generations. In the presence of atoms no less than in the presence of the infinities above us, we moderate our exaggerated self-importance. We gain a detachment from the overwhelming ego, and that is a first step to a fair appraisal and understanding of personalities other than our own.

These, then, are some of the reasons why the study in college of the liberal arts and sciences seems to me to prepare men for a less self-centered and miserly existence, for an attitude of mind which will seek the good of one in the good of all.

Let us pass on to the studies of the professional schools, and first of these to the study of law. The legal profession has always embodied the heights and depths of moral quality. It has had its foxes and its lions. A rising standard of requirements for admission to the bar has tended, in recent years, to correct the evils which have harassed and distressed the honorable members of the profession. But some of those evils have at the same time been accentuated. What may we expect as regards the ethics of legal practice when the study of the law, throughout the land, has been securely placed on a university footing?

The question is unanswerable, in any absolute terms. There will still be unregenerate rascals, no doubt, who will use the light to produce smoke and shadows. But they will know and their associates will know that they are sinning against the light. These liberalized university courses in jurisprudence are showing clearly that the long history of human legislation and litigation, in spite of all vagaries, is making toward the establishment of justice in the world of men; and that justice is the permanent good of all as opposed to the temporary advantage of individuals. When the majesty of this movement has dawned upon our students of law, when they have come to know somewhat of the dominant personalities of bench and bar all through the contentious life of the ages, when they find their impersonal studies in the sciences centering upon the mastery of proof and evidence in the relation of man to man and that in an age when science is so largely influential in human affairs, then they will have gained a view of life and its obligations that no experience of life in its baser manifestations "can utterly abolish or destroy." The pettiness of small practice and the more subtle temptations of great causes cannot erase from their memory the vision of a world in which great minds have spent the utmost of their power that the selfishness and passion of the few shall not subvert the good of all.

We come next to studies of the medical group. It is here that the natural sciences concentrate upon the making of human vigor and the alleviation of human suffering. It is not too much to say that, the more scientific these approaches become, so much the more the medical profession is detached from a sordid professionalism. Such detachment may be secured only by prolonged and mighty effort. The struggle to that end is still going on in American medicine and dentistry, with professional and governmental agencies successfully cooperating. But governments can go no farther than they can secure public support, and these professions cannot bring that support for measures mainly directed to the private advantage of their membership. In the long run, the hope of a fully stabilized medical practice must depend upon the assurance and conviction that that practice is working for public ends by sound and unassailable means. The malpractice of incompetent practitioners hurts the common cause. It is equally true that narrow self-seeking on the part of competent practitioners weakens the common cause. No university can guarantee that its professional graduates will all of them be professional in the higher sense. But a university has gone a long way in that direction when it has aroused in its students an interest in pure science and in the application of pure science to human needs, particularly when it has added thereto such teaching of the humanities as makes for broad appreciations in human life.

The profession of engineering shares the preëminence of the medical group as a vocation resting upon scientific knowledge. The products of engineering are subject to even more obvious and spectacular tests than those of medicine. If a road is badly built, it soon crumbles. If a bridge is unsound, it soon gives way. Where mechanical accuracy plays so large a part it would not be strange if human relationships were subordinated. One reason, I think, why the members of the engineering profession so often play subordinate parts and receive only secondary rewards, even while civilization is marching to its triumphs over structures of their making, is that the personal aspects of their undertakings are so largely held in abeyance.

The first business of an engineer is unquestionably that he be accurate and reliable. A profession that embodies these virtues is contributing fundamental elements to the moral life of our people. We see this all about us. Hundreds of structures every year are rising hundreds of feet into the air. How rarely does any radical defect of construction appear. Ten thousand automobiles pass in an hour with no breakdown due to faulty construction. Telephones by the hundred thousand are in constant use, and, when a single one of them fails, the users feel that they have been outraged. Competent engineering is spread out everywhere, all over our

ONE AND ALL

daily life, and the honesty of it is one of the moral aspects of the nation.

But the more personal and social aspects of the profession call also for emphasis. Fortunately, out of the ranks of the engineers who invent and construct, there are arising here and there great leaders of the profession, who view it in its human relationships, and carry its soundness and its inventiveness into vast undertakings for the good of all.

Is American genius equal to the task of taming our own Mississippi River? Some months ago, I ventured to say that this problem put to a supreme test both the political and the scientific quality of our people. Thanks largely to President Coolidge, to his mental and moral integrity, the first political perils of this undertaking have been fairly met. There will be others to follow, but we have now ground for hope that American engineering will have the chance to show its mettle in this stupendous task. Other tasks are coming on in which the engineering profession will be our main reliance for great contributions to the general welfare. As such undertakings grow in magnitude, they involve coöperation with other professions, with all of the professions. If those who are called to these large responsibilities shall keep themselves clear of political activity in its baser forms, of partisan and personal intrigue, and shall make of their employment a genuine public service, they will know some of the finest satisfactions of those who have learned to find their good in furtherance of the common good.

We come now to a group of occupations which belong to the higher levels of human interest, but are not yet fully recognized as professions.

And what then is a profession? I think it is an occupation which makes use of organized knowledge for public ends. It

A FEW REMARKS

is more than this, to be sure. It has traditions. It has accepted procedures and an ethics of its own. It has a body of practitioners who stand for these things, and a literature in which these things are embodied. But fundamentally it is an occupation which makes use of established and organized and advancing knowledge with a dominant concern for the general good.

A calling, however important and indispensable, will not be recognized as a profession so long as it has no abiding concern for the common weal. It is only by emphasis upon its contribution to the good of all that it can attain to such recognition. But the more thoroughly any one of these occupations is studied with reference to its basis of organized knowledge—the more scientific its procedure becomes—so much the more is it revealed as having an underlying and a necessary relation to the general good. So much the more will its educated practitioners take account of the effect of its operations upon the welfare of the community. This is true of all of our major pursuits in the field of industry and commerce.

Accordingly, the universities, in educating for business, are inevitably accentuating the trend of business toward a professional status. They are basing their teaching upon an economics which takes account of historic, social, and moral elements, as among its scientific data. They are penetrating into the psychology of men's relations with their fellow men in all that pertains to their economic life. A student must be extraordinarily impervious or morally blind if he can go through a modern university course in preparation for a business career without having borne in upon him the conception that in commercial life the good of one is bound up with the good of many and ultimately with the good of all.

The graduate in commerce who goes forth with this conception ingrained in his educated consciousness will find himself to that extent prepared to coöperate with the men who today are transforming American business practice to make it more effectively promote the general welfare. An influential expression of this trend in the business world is to be found in the code of "Principles of Business Conduct" adopted four years ago by the Chamber of Commerce of the United States. I quote from the text of this pronouncement:

> The function of business is to provide for the material needs of mankind, and to increase the wealth of the world and the value and happiness of life. . . . When business enterprise is successfully carried on with constant and efficient endeavor to reduce the cost of production and distribution, to improve the quality of its products, and to give fair treatment to customers, capital, management, and labor, it renders public service of the highest value.

The first of the principles following this preamble reads as follows: "The foundation of business is confidence, which springs from integrity, fair dealing, efficient service, and mutual benefit."

One of the most commanding institutions in the world today is the public press, its activities ramifying into every other manifestation of social life. The progress of journalism as a rising profession is similarly marked by the endeavor to formulate and stabilize the ethical standards of its practitioners. A significant example is found in the "Canons of Journalism" adopted some four or five years ago by the American Society of Newspaper Editors. The statement introductory to these canons reads as follows:

> The primary function of newspapers is to communicate to the human race what its members do, feel, and think. Journalism, therefore, demands of its practitioners the widest range of intelligence, of knowledge, and of experience, as well as natural and trained powers of observation and reasoning. To its opportunities as a chronicle are indissolubly linked its obligations as teacher and interpreter.

A FEW REMARKS

I have not touched upon all of the basic subjects of university education. Some of them deal more directly with the interdependence of men, and with the moral implications of such interdependence, than do those which I have mentioned. The social sciences are of this order. Still more, the philosophical sciences, particularly ethics and the philosophy of religion.

So, too, among the professions for which universities prepare, there are those which proceed more directly to the understanding and practice of life for the common good: the educational profession for one, and the ministry of religion. We might add what is vaguely known as the vocation of social welfare, in its multifarious forms. It goes without saying that these all point directly to that good of the one which is to be found in the good of all. But does it go without saying? Theoretically, yes. In the best examples, yes. But there are difficulties here, unlooked for difficulties. We cannot forget that the direct approach to moral good has dangers of its own which are often overlooked. Strange it may be, but experience shows that goodness itself—goodness beyond that which comes to a man through his heredity—is often a by-product of other interests in life. To the direct assault it is well-nigh as elusive as happiness. So the man whose very occupation in life is one directed to the betterment of mankind is subject to perils beyond those which beset pursuits of a less aspiring character. The professional moralist is peculiarly in need of the stern checks and balances of science, and of the wide horizons of history and the classical humanities. In furnishing these checks and widening these horizons, university education may sometimes dull the edge of moral enthusiasm. That is a result to be deplored in any life in which the earlier enthusiasm was genuine. But I have no question that, in the large, the result is otherwise. By rendering judgments farther-sighted, more tolerant, more secure, by relating single acts to large and fertile principles, such education increases the sum total of sustained endeavor for the betterment of the world.

I have spoken of the moral gains that are reached by indirection. Let me carry that thought now a little farther. The Greeks set forth the objects of spiritual striving as the good, the true, the beautiful, these three. Of these, the good is often found to be a function, as it were, of the beautiful and the true. Perhaps each of them is a function of the other two, but that question would take us too far afield for today. The good, at least, is dependent upon the true; and is it not equally dependent upon the beautiful? Not that taste may serve as a substitute for conscience. That we cannot admit. The venture in that direction is sure to bring disappointment. Beauty can no more lord it over morals than morals can determine the principles of art; but no more can either of them ignore the fellowship and influence of the other.

So, as the fine arts take their place in closer intimacy beside the sciences in our colleges, it is fair to expect that they will have part in that stream of university influence which turns men away from individual selfishness to a larger concern for the good of all. Music may be a miserly indulgence to the man or woman who is hopelessly self-centered, but no words can tell what enlargement it may bring to those who by nature find some room for the thought of their fellow men. And along with music, painting, sculpture at its best, architecture, poetry, and the rest of that glorious company have shown a power to move upon responsive spirits whose aspiration would never have dared so far but for those free utterances of loftier minds.

It may seem that what I have thus far discussed comes back

to an "enlightened selfishness," and nothing more. That may be so, but I think that is not all. I have noticed in human life that an enlightened selfishness when sufficiently enlightened eventuates in much the same conduct as an idealistic theory when it grapples with actualities. From whatever side the general problem of ethics is approached, if the approach is of a seriousness appropriate to university studies, the outcome shows the fundamental impossibility of isolating the interests of the individual from those of the social organism in which he has his being. The circle of any good which may come to him in this life is embraced within the larger circle of social good.

Jesus drove this home in a way of his own. A lawyer had quoted to him those golden words from the book of *Leviticus*, "Thou shalt love thy neighbor as thyself," and had followed them with the penetrating question, "Who is my neighbor?" His reply was the parable of the Good Samaritan.

Whoever needs the help that I can give, he is my neighbor. That is the teaching of the parable. And so this simple tale has come down through the ages, obscured by the arrogance and bigotry and violence of men, but shining with a clear and steady light. In that light, there can be no absolute limit to any man's concern for the good of his fellow man.

But here a problem arises that cannot be disregarded. To what circle shall a man give the main activity and allegiance of his life? We cannot spread our benevolence equally and continuously over all the world. No man is large enough for that. Some concentration there must be if we would avoid mere thin abstraction, sentiment, futility. At this point appear some of the most critical decisions that we have to face in life. Some of you, no doubt, are facing such decisions this very day. Opposing claims appeal to you. Shall you follow the larger good, and lose the finer good which is near at hand? Or shall you seize upon that which is near at hand and renounce your larger hope and destiny?

Sometimes the opposition of claims assumes the bitterness of open conflict. Then you must choose either the wider or the narrower allegiance and defend your choice even with your life. Such was the case with the men of the South at the outbreak of the Civil War. The burden of decision fell with peculiar force upon those officers of the Army and Navy whose home was in the northern tier of the Southern States. Should it be loyalty to their Country or loyalty to their State—for a time had come when it could not be both at once. Lee and Stonewall Jackson went with their State against the Union of States. Farragut and George H. Thomas went each against his State and took their stand with the Union. High-minded men, all of them, men inflexibly devoted to duty as they saw it; men whose hearts were wrung by the hard necessity of that choice.

You, too, will have choices to make which may be as critical in their way as these were to the men of our Civil War. There is no single formula that can settle for you, out of hand, these questions as they arise in your life. You cannot simply choose the larger unit and be sure that that is best. Sometimes the smaller circle embraces the larger good. You cannot make your choice by formulæ, but in the long run your choice will show what men you are and what your education has done for you.

While education has given you no infallible rules, it has taught you some things that will stand by you when you are in the valley of decision. Let me mention two of these. For one thing, you have learned in some measure to know yourselves, and that may help you to choose between the larger

A FEW REMARKS

circle and the smaller circle as the scene of your particular activities. In the second place, you have gained some outlook on the larger good, the good of the larger circle, the good of all. However concentrated your interests may in time become, you can never again quite shut that window upon the world of your fellow men. Your education, if it has struck home, has unfitted you to be simple egoists. You must indeed concentrate upon one primary concern in life. But you will not let that concentration taper you down utterly to its restricted compass. Rather will it appear that your special circle —family, job, institution, profession—will enlarge somewhat in the range of its sympathies and services for the quality of life that you will put into its life.

X

THE DUTY OF THINKING

*From the Baccalaureate Address delivered at
University Heights, June 6, 1926*

X

THE DUTY OF THINKING

DO we not mistake a mere mental habit for serious thinking? Men are by nature either *yea* or *nay*. Put to one man a new project, a new conception, a new candidate for favor, and he votes *no* on the instant. It is his nature to vote *no*. Put the same to another man, and he votes *aye* on the instant. It is his nature to vote *aye*. He is carried away by an appeal for his approval. A more sluggish nature will put off an answer altogether, rather than incur the pain of decision. Some are unhappy unless they are with the majority. Some are unhappy unless they are in a minority. Some are against change, in their very blood and bone. Some are for change, any change whatsoever. And others are for sleep.

But if the matter is of any consequence, the inborn conservative should think it out before he answers *no*. The inborn radical should think it out before he answers *aye*. The sluggard should take whip and spur to his mind, till it gives an answer or gives adequate reason for postponement.

All three of us, *yea* and *nay* and *mañana,* what credit we take to ourselves for an answer which is merely our old nature repeating itself by rote! There is nothing to praise in such a reply. It has no moral quality. Men are not moral till they rule themselves to the extent of doing better than they would do by nature.

Both indolence and self-approval combine to maintain our thought at an established level. That is a besetting sin of educated men who have bought their education and set it away to keep. The glorious thing is to change our minds and give adequate reason for the change; or else to hold fast to our old conviction for a better reason, when the old reasons have lost their authority. Both are exhilarating and worthy of a man.

The born conservatives of our times cannot afford to let all of the thinking be done by the born radicals of our time. They should, at least, give their opponents a run for their money, and shake down the pennyweight of gold from their mountain weight of eloquence. The born radicals cannot afford to go on sounding the old, unchanging phrases, till they become a mere revolutionary formula, an orthodoxy of discontent.

Both are necessary, if our age is to have its enlightenment and progress. But the age will not have the enlightenment which is its due, unless both conservatives and radicals shall think their way out, some two or three parasangs at least, beyond their present encampment. On the next stage, they may find themselves not so hopelessly at variance. They may even swell the ranks of those who do the major work of the world, somewhere between the easy and irresponsible extremes.

Just now there has come to my desk a new book which will illustrate my meaning. It is by Edwin Mims, and bears the title, *The Advancing South*. I would not accept it throughout. Who would accept any book throughout? But I have not seen any other recent volume which presents so concretely, temperately, convincingly, the spread of fresh and wholesome thinking through great areas of hereditary conservatism.

Professor Mims recognizes the unquestionable value to the nation of the conservative tradition of the South. He recognizes, too, the likelihood that reaction from that tradition may

THE DUTY OF THINKING

lead to individual excesses, freakish, cynical, and anarchistic, as it has led, North as well as South. But the picture which he presents, of a South reawakening in spirit, renewing that other American tradition of free insight and free discussion, is reassuring and inspiring. It is a book of personalities. While it has no declared connection with those incredible proceedings at Dayton, Tennessee, it may nevertheless serve toward a revision of the belittling view of Southern ideas which the Scopes trial spread abroad to all the world. This book represents a South which is doing its own thinking, regardless of Mr. Bryan or Mr. Clarence Darrow, and as far from the one as from the other; a South that is taking thought for the continuous and constructive betterment of its life.

"The weak point in the literary armour of the South," says Professor Mims, "is the lack of satire—the inability to laugh at itself." Yes, and that is the weak point of Puritanism, that other great, formative conservatism of our American life. But another native American strain is supplying this lack, and supplying it to excess. The ability to laugh is a saving salt in our way of thinking. That is not to be forgotten. But the craving for laughter is coming to be ridiculous. Broadway is scrambling after new forms of fun. "A hundred laughs in a hundred minutes" is not enough. And our comic papers—what a blessing it would be if they appeared only at irregular intervals, like the real laughs in real life, and only when they had assembled enough of genuine pleasantries to fill their columns. College comics might set the example.

But not a word against genuine fun or genuine caricature. That is precious. That is indispensable. Any long-continued thought, except the toughest and the mightiest, would soon go stale without it.

But what do we mean by thought? Is it logic or is it wisdom? Again and again we shall find logic on the one side of a question and wisdom on the other. Logic is elemental, necessary, something akin to duty in the realm of pure intellect. But in politics, you embalm a man when you call him "the logical candidate." Wisdom is more—humanity, insight, taste, catholicity — whatever it may be, it is beyond dialectic and formulæ, it still responds to the rein but its power is its own.

Cardinal Newman, supreme logician that he was, declared against "that vague thing called . . . 'our common Christianity.' " "I discard it," he said, "for the very reason that it cannot throw itself into a proposition." Undoubtedly religion has its propositions, which are essential to its organized life, but it is more, immeasurably more. I should rather agree with others of the same faith, or with Cardinal Newman himself when he sings, "Lead, Kindly Light," and discard any religion that can be completely and finally thrown into propositions. Some part of all true wisdom is imagination. To be wise, you must know more than you can prove. You may become a useful draughtsman or analyst if your thought runs constantly along straight lines and geometric angles; but the way to become a leader of men—that is another trail. The straight lines and right angles are indispensable, to be sure, but how are they to take their place in the arena of humanity? The directions are not in the books. To be wise, you must learn for yourselves what it is to be wise. You must take your risk of mistake. It is glory enough for your college if it has guarded you against some of the risks which are the delight of fools, and has lessened by so much your percentage of probable error.

But the interest of your college goes beyond your individual careers, into the modest part which you shall have in the spread of wisdom among our American people. Here, again, no formula can suffice. Our people will make mistakes, as

THE DUTY OF THINKING

individuals will make mistakes. The method is that of trial and error. But our institutions of learning will not have done all that they should do unless the American people shall become a people capable of taking second thought. In the broad and large, this people has not gone fatally wrong hitherto. But our immeasurable prosperity and success in many directions renders it the more imperative that we become a people acting, not upon instant emotion and impulse, but upon matured intelligence and moral purpose.

It is possible that second thoughts might have prevented our Civil War and the miseries which followed. They might have found other cure for the evils of the time. No man can say. But it is certain that such deliberation, to have been successful, must have come abroad among our people before the spirit of '61 had reached its culmination. I believe the second thoughts of our people might have found ways of preventing the Spanish War without loss to the higher interests of humanity. As regards the World War, we cannot be accused of lack of deliberation. But the war was on already, and our deliberation ceased to be a virtue. Nevertheless, our long-delayed decision at that time is evidence that America will not be hurried into war in the crises of the future. We may have to fight again. The contingency is not impossible. But we will not fight on the drop of the hat. We shall take second thought and thought from every angle. What is more to the point, we shall take thought in time: and the time is now. We shall take thought to forestall the causes of war, to the greater glory of the Nation and the greater good of mankind. But do not let the American people forget that the time to prevent the next war is now, now, now. Not by extravagance of anti-war emotion, for the very extravagance against war at this moment may turn to extravagance for war in an actual crisis. Not by emotional extravagance of any kind, but by taking thought when it is forethought, may the American people stabilize and advance those practical measures which look to international justice and collaboration in the place of international war. Through the World Court, through concerted measures toward disarmament, through definition and suppression of aggressive warfare, they have to think their way and make their way to abiding peace, while there is yet time, in these days of an unstable peace.

But let us come back to more individual aspects, and consider next and last the materials of your thought. I have in mind two classes of materials. As a modern thinker, you must make use of modern science. You must equally make use of ancient letters. The first is obvious, the second is paradoxical.

No man can know the whole of modern science. Yet we are to live in a world of scientific knowledge, and that world is changing from day to day. How shall we keep our bearings? It is, in effect, the question proposed not long ago by President Frank of the University of Wisconsin, and sent forth with all the urgency of S O S. There is no easy answer. One must keep alive to change; one must cultivate respect for the specialist, so long as he utters his oracles from his own temple; one must avoid becoming ridiculous either from lack of knowledge or from conceit of knowledge; one must learn the steadfastness of suspended judgment while the evidence is coming in; one must act on part knowledge, when action cannot wait. There is no universal rule. But in one way and another, the general intelligence goes on making those readjustments which the advance of science demands.

You will make use of modern science, but none the less you will make use of ancient letters. Why ancient? Because of vitality. There is vitality, no doubt, in the writings of our own

THE DUTY OF THINKING

time. It is not to be ignored. But it has not been sifted by the centuries. However, it is not merely time that decides. It is the generations of men. The spirit of mankind has swung its flail through all manner of conflict, heartbreak, novelty, futility, unbearable monotony, and gleams of triumph, slow threshing, threshing out its golden grain. The spirit of the race, your own spirit, is in no small part what has survived in the books and the traditions of the race. They are the soil from which you have sprung. You renew your own essential life when you plant your feet upon that soil. You would be the better for it if every day, besides your morning paper, you were to read from the living books of the ages. They are not old. Having survived the past, they belong to the future. Your great-grandchildren will read them with the thrill of a new inspiration. What else they may read we cannot guess, but if they live a civilized life they will know Homer and Plato and Sophocles; they will know Dante and Shakespeare and Milton. Their world interest, widening out beyond our own, may well include the ancient writings of Chinese and Indian masters, but the masters of our own classical antiquity will inevitably be theirs.

So, if you will have it so, your own thought will renew its strength from day to day. And let no supercilious prejudice keep you from reading those other masterpieces, the Hebrew and Christian Scriptures. They are little known because they are so familiar. Yet they, too, have a life that will not die. They are supremely immortal. The modern world is permeated with their imagery and their ideas. You will use them, even if unconsciously and at secondhand. But if you have acquaintance with them, direct and unconventional intercourse with them, they will lend their fruit and flavor to your daily life.

XI

DEAN RUSSELL'S QUARTER CENTURY

An Address at the Alumni Conference at Teachers College, Columbia University, February 22, 1923, Celebrating the Completion by Dr. James E. Russell of Twenty-five Years in the Deanship of the College

XI

DEAN RUSSELL'S QUARTER CENTURY

THE training of teachers in this country began on a lower academic level than that of the colleges. It took a prophet to anticipate such instruction in our higher institutions of learning. New York University, as early as 1830, called one of these prophets to be professor of the philosophy of education. If Thomas H. Gallaudet had not had other plans, this would have marked the beginning. Eventually, that early morning dream of the founders was realized in New York University's pioneer School of Pedagogy, now known as the School of Education.

Half a century after this fruitless call to Dr. Gallaudet, another of the major prophets, President F. A. P. Barnard, was sounding his call for the higher education of teachers. It was a significant utterance, but so far as the East was concerned, it came as a voice in the wilderness. Meanwhile, farther West, the state universities had begun to feel a pedagogical impulse. In the seventies and the early eighties half a dozen of them had established departments of education. Of these, the most influential was undoubtedly that of the University of Michigan, under Professor William H. Payne and, later, Professor B. A. Hinsdale.

It was during the eighties that the germ of Teachers College was sprouting and sending out its tentative tendrils in many directions. Like many another interesting beginning, in art and education, it hovered about the region of Washington Square. After a time it came under the leadership of a promising and enterprising young graduate of Columbia College bearing the name of Nicholas Murray Butler, and soon it was found gravitating in the direction of Columbia University. Or shall we say that Columbia gravitated toward Teachers College. They were both of them younger, smaller, and more impressionable than they are today. There is a tradition that Teachers College came first to Morningside Heights and that the University followed after. With all of their intimate association, there was a certain shyness between them, a certain willingness to rest content with a Platonic rather than a matrimonial connection, to say nothing of a relationship like that of a foster parent to an orphan child, adopted into the family. But maybe this is ground where even angels should fear to tread. Anyway, there is no one to question that Teachers College is now and has been for many years a member of the Columbia family. It came definitely into the "educational system of Columbia University"—I use the official phraseology—in that same year in which Dr. Russell became its Dean.

We shall detract not at all from Dean Russell's glory, if we recognize the fact that a tremendous work had been accomplished here before he came into his deanship. We shall detract not at all from the achievements of his predecessors, if we declare that the real Teachers College, as we know it, had hardly even begun to be when he came into his deanship. The real Teachers College is his opus, his masterpiece. He has made it by consolidating and widening the distinguished company of its friends and supporters. But chiefly he has made it by building up a notable faculty—an organized, cohesive, and creative faculty. To make such a faculty, you must bring together a group of strong professors, each of them with

DEAN RUSSELL'S QUARTER CENTURY

a mind of his own, and weld them into a brotherhood, with a corporate mind of its own. If you think this an easy undertaking!—well, you can only tell by trying. When you see such a phenomenon, however, do not ascribe it all to the heavenly-mindedness of those professors, but to him who has persuaded them to keep on being heavenly-minded.

Look at the Columbia catalogue for 1897–98, with its list of eighteen members of the faculty of Teachers College. The most of the names are familiar ones today. Professor Baker is there; so are Professor Dodge and Miss Baldwin. So is James Earl Russell, half way down the list and designated as professor of psychology and general method. That was 1897–98. Then here we have the catalogue of 1907–08, ten years later, with its ninety-two names instead of eighteen in the list of the Teachers College faculty. Nicholas Murray Butler, president; James Earl Russell, dean; Clyde Furst, secretary. Look over the names of the professors and make note of the names that did not appear in that earlier list. You can easily point to a dozen who are known today throughout our American educational system, all of them added within those first ten years of Dean Russell's administration. There is Frank M. McMurry, our acknowledged master of the art of classroom instruction; there is Edward L. Thorndike, who has made mathematics a branch of psychology, along with David Eugene Smith, who has made psychology and everything else a branch of mathematics; there is Gonzalez Lodge, for whom Latin and Greek are still the sovereign lords of American education, and alongside of him is Dr. Wood, for whom the sum of classical wisdom is *mens sana in sano corpore* —he sings the phrase crescendo; there is Julius Sachs, master of secondary education in both theory and practice; there is Maurice A. Bigelow, on the way to a directorship in practical

A FEW REMARKS

arts; there is Miss Adelaide Nutting, who lends distinction to every phase of the subject of her instruction; there is John Dewey, whose philosophy has permeated and stimulated, not to say bewitched, this whole establishment, as well as the rest of mankind; there is Samuel Train Dutton—if you care to see how one man put out at interest every talent that his Maker gave him, filling his seventy years with service of mankind, you have only to read Charles Herbert Levermore's life of Dr. Samuel T. Dutton; there are David Snedden and Henry Suzzallo, who came on from Stanford University, and there is George Strayer, from nearer home—the marks of their influence are to be found far and wide in the educational systems of this country; there is Paul Monroe—the College and the whole educational world have been enriched by his contribution.

It is only because of limitations of time that the enumeration must stop at this point. You will note, moreover, that I have taken no account of additions made in the past fifteen years, including such hopeful youngsters as W. C. Bagley, Milo Hillegas, and William H. Kilpatrick. The latest catalogue shows a Teachers College faculty of well over two hundred members.

It is clear that Dean Russell has been keeping a lookout for men. He has shown none of the weakness of a third-rate administrator, who is fearful of being eclipsed by his associates. He has never been found looking anxiously into some mirror of public opinion to see that his halo is on straight. But his associates have no illusions. They know their leader. It is this that has kept men of such strength and independence working as a united faculty. It is this that has made such men willing to become members of the faculty of Teachers College.

It is worth while to remark the change in the main function

DEAN RUSSELL'S QUARTER CENTURY

of Teachers College which has come with the building up of a faculty of marked initiative and leadership. Not only has it extended its activities in many directions, but it has come to be preëminently, not a college for teachers, but a college for the teachers of teachers and for the overseers of teachers. As a natural accompaniment, it has ceased to be mainly a school of instruction and has become, in increasing measure, a school of research. It has accordingly become one of the chief contributors to our newer literature of education.

When I undertook to organize the department of education in the University of California, in a former generation, that is, in 1892, there was a modest sum available to start a pedagogical section in the University library. A portion of this sum was expended in the purchase of works in French and German, but I did not wish to overload the shelves with what the majority of my students could read only with difficulty if at all. Then I was put to it to make a justifiable expenditure of even the few hundred dollars remaining. Many of the volumes ordered, although standard handbooks of the teaching profession, made a trivial showing as compared with the collections in agriculture, engineering, jurisprudence, and other professional subjects. For use in the classroom there was nothing available that could be compared with the texts of the older professions. We had, to be sure, Professor Payne's translation of Compayré's *History of Pedagogy*, a comparatively new work at that time, along with Quick's *Educational Reformers;* we had Spencer's *Education,* Bain's *Education as a Science,* and some thoroughly sensible volumes on the practice of teaching in elementary schools. I remember that, aside from Professor Payne's little volume on *School Supervision,* our main reliance in the field of administration was the report on *City School Systems* prepared by John D. Philbrick. When

A FEW REMARKS

the *Report of the Committee of Ten* appeared, in 1894, it provided the best text then available for the study of secondary education.

I have no desire to exaggerate the poverty of this literature. There was, as you know, a mass of pedagogical writings already extant in English, and it contained, here and there, works of such weight and distinction as would be hard to match in more recent publications. Even the past decade has not been prolific in educational classics. Pestalozzi and Froebel were there in translation and commentary. Herbart was just dawning upon the English-speaking world. Dr. William T. Harris was in the full tide of his influence. His *Psychologic Foundations of Education*, however, did not appear until 1898. President G. Stanley Hall was leading in a new psychological approach to education, which aroused and sometimes bewildered the teaching fraternity. But with all of this philosophical and psychological utterance, the conspicuous lack was on the side of the social aspects of education. Our methodology was based on an individualistic psychology, of one sort or another. Our educational history was mainly the history of opinion rather than of institutions.

Now, Teachers College has not invented the social view of education, but it has been in all of its main departments a conspicuous exponent of that view. How much of our newer literature of educational institutions and institutional life has come from this source? I cannot say; but I would venture the guess that more than half of it is the work of men and women either connected with Teachers College or distinctly influenced by Teachers College.

In its volume and in its erudition this literature is impressive as compared with the mass of what had been produced in the preceding generation. It has provided a respectable equipment of working tools for the training of the teaching profession. From Paul Monroe's *History* and *Cyclopedia of Education* out in all directions this work has made an unmistakable impress on American education. It has gone far to render our teaching in secondary schools and our supervision of elementary schools a professional occupation.

Dean Russell's personal attitude as a cheerful crusader has gone far to consolidate the position of schools and departments of education in other universities. These schools and departments have been built up in the face of simply unbelievable distrust and opposition in the academic world. Having made this one professional college for teachers unquestionably a going concern, and knowing well the progress making at other centers, this Dean has not hesitated to affirm that professional standards and professional training in the pedagogical field are already *fait accompli;* that the obvious deficiencies on the side of the teaching profession are unhappily matched with equally glaring deficiencies on the part of the older professions; and that education is advancing with the others, and as rapidly as any, toward the scientific determination of its practice.

Back in the beginning of his career, his first significant contribution to educational literature was a volume entitled *German Higher Schools.* That was twenty-five years ago, but the book is so characteristic of the man that it seems worth while to recall it today. It has not been superseded, in fact, by any later work in English on this subject. It represents "almost five years' continuous study and investigation," two of which had been passed in Germany, visiting schools in more than forty towns and cities, and consulting personally with many of the foremost leaders of German secondary education. It is remarkably comprehensive, but it is enlivened with carefully

A FEW REMARKS

studied detail, by way of illustration. It has no trace of propaganda, and approval and disapproval are distributed with the greatest impartiality.

I evidently read the book from cover to cover soon after it appeared; for when I took my copy down from its shelf yesterday to look through it again, I found my pencil markings spotting the margin of every chapter, if not of every page; and at the end I had written the date, November 8, 1899.

Indeed, I liked the book so much, both inside and out, that when I had a manuscript of my own made ready, I went to the same publisher and asked him to issue my book in the same style—crown octavo, with corresponding page and type, with the same binding in green linen cloth. It was as shameless a proceeding as that of a woman copying another woman's millinery. But the young Dean took it all in good part; and so his maiden effort and my maiden effort, hand in hand, have come merrily down the years together.

This is only one recollection of friendly relationships, out of many, running back more than a quarter of a century, which render my contribution to this symposium a tribute of personal affection.

There is one great lack from which Teachers College suffers today, and that lack I would gladly supply if possible. I mean the lack of adequate competition. It is lonesome for an institution to tower so far above others of its kind. There is a lack of zest when there is no close second, which may any day step into the leading place. We are not able at New York University to offer such a rival at the present moment. But we are on the way; and Dean Withers, in his genuine affection for Teachers College, may be counted on in the next ten years to do all that can be done to provide you with an active competitor. I am going to help to the best of my ability, for the

DEAN RUSSELL'S QUARTER CENTURY

interests of Teachers College are dear to my heart, and I would not willingly leave this thing undone, which is so necessary to her spiritual good.

Or, to speak more judicially, since competition in the field of education is an absurdity or worse: We shall do all in our power to give you a good running mate, right here at home. We are grateful for the help we have received from Teachers College; we shall help all we can in return; and we look forward with happy anticipation to the years of friendly relationship which stretch out before these two institutions, in our home town, at these crossroads of the world.

XII

ARTIST MECHANICS

From an Address to the Graduates of the School Department of The General Society of Mechanics and Tradesmen, New York City, delivered at the School, April 12, 1922

XII

ARTIST MECHANICS

I HASTEN to discuss, in light and inadequate fashion, a subject in which I am keenly interested, namely, certain ways in which art enters the daily task of every man, ways in which every kind of workman, industrial, commercial, or professional, has to be more or less of an artist. Let me give two very homely and humble illustrations of the thing I have in mind.

In the city of Washington, I went hurriedly one day into the barber shop at the New Willard Hotel. When I had slipped into a chair, I asked the presiding barber if he would trim my hair and beard in fifteen minutes. He answered very deliberately, "Yes, I can do it, but the time is really too short. To get a good job, the barber must look at his customer's head and picture to himself just how that head should look when he is through with it. Then he should make it look that way, no matter how much time it takes." Needless to say, I compromised and gave him all the time I could spare. Needless also to add that while he did not produce a result of surpassing beauty—there were reasons why that was impossible—he did give me a better trim than I could usually command. And, what was better, he gave me food for thought in the half hour I spent in his chair.

At the opposite extremity, I had another lesson years ago. I was at the time a visitor in the city of New York. As I walked these streets, one of my well-worn shoes suddenly gave out and required immediate attention. I went into one of the Cammeyer stores—it was pretty well down on Sixth Avenue then—bought a fresh pair, left the others to be mended, and went forth in my new finery to look for a bootblack. The stand which I found had only one chair, and there was no waiting line of customers. The little Italian proprietor apparently had time to do his work according to his own standard of excellence. He promptly gave me a perfectly good shine. Then he looked at it critically and smeared it all out again. This was repeated four times over before I received a dignified dismissal. As I went away I turned back for a last look at my new Italian friend. There he stood gazing intently at my feet. He had paid little attention to the coin I had placed in his hand. He cared not a rap who or what I was or who or what I was not. He was not impressed by the fact that I had a pair of perfectly new shoes. He was simply looking on the work of his own hands. He looked upon it lovingly, and saw that it was good.

Now, the greater part of what I want to say tonight is told by that Italian bootblack and that Washington barber. It is a matter of the highest concern to all of us that the spirit of those two workmen shall be the spirit of workmen everywhere, from the highest grade to the lowest: that they shall put themselves into their work; that they shall be interested, first of all, in the thing done and not in the pay for doing it; that they shall be willing to give time and toil, as much as may be necessary, as the price of perfection, or of their possible approach to perfection; that they shall have an ideal and follow it, whether they are working under orders or free to "gang their ain gait." So shall they be artists as far as their occupation goes, and so shall they contribute something to the higher life of their time.

ARTIST MECHANICS

I shall doubtless be told that machinery has ruled all initiative out of the modern workshop, that if an artisan tries to be an artist, even a little bit of an artist, he will simply lose his job. That is only half-way true. So far as it is true it is a problem for modern corporation personnel psychology, and a very serious problem. But even in the most modern shops there is a chance for men who have the instinct for higher workmanship. How great a chance there is will appear from the recent writings of Mr. Charles M. Schwab, which tell of his own experience with workmen who look beyond their pay.

There comes to mind a very different illustration of the creative instinct of an artist in every-day business. It is to be found in a work of fiction which attracted wide attention some twenty years ago. It was written by George H. Lorimer, now editor of the *Saturday Evening Post*. The book was the *Letters from a Self-made Merchant to his Son*. The merchant tells the story of Jim Durham. Jim had come to the merchant for a job. He was not unknown, for the merchant had had business dealings with the young man's father, in which the father had come out second best. But Jim had a double handicap. He was invincibly lazy, and he was a college graduate. The merchant proceeded to get rid of him by setting him at hard manual labor, loading beef on the cars. Jim stuck to the task manfully for a time; then it began to bore him; and he set his wits to work to abolish it. He devised an overhead trolley to carry the beef, without the expenditure of human muscle. By this means he invented himself out of a job.

But the invention saved the concern a lot of money, so they could not in decency set the inventor adrift. They gave him a place as timekeeper. This was dull work, but before long he had a machine introduced for registering the time of the men. The machine did away with the most of the timekeepers,

A FEW REMARKS

including Jim. It was a money-saver for the company, and they simply had to give him something else to do. He was taken into the office to copy circular letters. Here again he tired of the monotony. He pestered the management into using typewriters, which were then a novelty. Very soon there was no more use for a longhand copyist; once again he had abolished his own job.

As a last resort, they sent him on the road to sell a new brand of beef extract. Here he hardly paid his traveling expenses, but he proceeded to show his boss that they were working on the wrong lines. They should prepare the way for the salesman by judicious advertising. If he had not been a success at selling beef extract, he could at least sell his idea of advertising to his own employer. They gave him a chance, and he threw himself into the new undertaking with unbounded enthusiasm. The new extract was advertised everywhere by all manner of happy and original devices. He got his girl to help him with recipes in which beef extract was indispensable. But the results were slow to follow. The costs piled up out of all proportion to the sales. The disproportion grew worse and worse, until Jim's dismissal from the service loomed near at hand. Then there came a slight improvement. Then more improvement, and the income was breaking even with the costs. Then the orders began to come in a flood, and Jim was finally landed in a permanent position in the establishment.

So much for the tale. I have read it again this week and found it as bright and breezy as it was twenty years ago.

The employers of these young draftsmen will not be grateful to me if I encourage them to substitute originality for fidelity. I shall not be found making such a mistake, if I lay due emphasis upon the fact that all art of lasting value unites greatness of form with greatness of imagination. There is

ARTIST MECHANICS

probably from age to age more evanescent art, more art that fails to survive, because of defect of form, than because of defect of originality. The noblest visions are worthy of the noblest vehicles to carry them down the ages. So the first lesson of an artist in any walk of life is subjection to the rules of his craft. In art as in government, no man is worthy to rule who has not learned to serve.

It was in the field of architectural draughtsmanship that I once had this truth brought home to me most forcibly. A great international competition was held some quarter-of-a-century ago for a general plan for the buildings and grounds of the University of California. The large expense of the undertaking was borne by that great and gracious dame, Mrs. Phebe A. Hearst. The commission of award, representing the Architectural Institute of America, assigned the first prize to M. E. Bénard, of Paris. There was much discussion regarding the rival merits of the plans as presented in the newspapers; but when the original drawings were all shown side by side at a public exhibition in the Ferry Building in San Francisco, there was no question as to the superior execution of the Bénard plans. For many a young draughtsman without European training, I believe these drawings set a new standard of perfection. Their fullness, their fineness and accuracy, had something to do in all likelihood with the favor which these plans won with the judges. Whatever modifications may have been made in later years under the masterly supervision of Mr. John Galen Howard, those first designs of M. Bénard have undoubtedly led the way in the great architectural development of that foremost of far western universities.

Let us turn to an American artist, and learn what we can from the way he made himself great. At Madison Square there are two fine examples of the work of Augustus Saint

A FEW REMARKS

Gaudens, the statue of Farragut, which faces Fifth Avenue, and the dainty figure of Diana on the tower of Madison Square Garden. At Fifth Avenue and Fifty-ninth Street there is another, which dignifies the entrance to Central Park, the notable Sherman group. This is statuary which, to my eye, does not grow old or familiar. I gaze upon these figures every time I pass, with a pleasure that is always new. When I go to Boston, I rarely miss a chance for one more look at another work of Saint Gaudens, the Shaw monument on the Common, across the street from the State House.

We have the story of the production of these great works delightfully told in *The Reminiscences of Augustus Saint-Gaudens,* edited by his son. It took the artist three years to produce the Farragut, and they were years of alternating hope and disgust. When near the end, he wrote to John La Farge, "My Farragut will soon be finished. . . . I haven't the faintest idea of the merit of what I have produced. At times I think it's good, then indifferent, then bad."

It was ten years from the time the Sherman monument was begun until it reached completion. The difficulties of the work had weighed upon him and he was extravagantly happy when they were overcome. "While I was at it," he wrote, "the days came and went rapidly because of my steady and enthusiastic toil." In an intimate letter to a friend he gave vent to his enthusiasm for the figure of Victory in this group: "My 'Victory' is getting on well. It's the grandest 'Victory' anybody ever made. Hooraah! and I shall have the model done in a month or so." After no end of trouble, the casting of the group was at last finished, and he wrote to his son, "Sometimes I'd cry, then I'd laugh, then I'd do both together, then I'd rush out into the street and howl, and so on. Now it's as peaceful as the ocean in a dead calm. Only I have got a swelled head for the first time in my life, for the 'Sherman' really looks bully and is smashingly fine."

It took fourteen years for Saint Gaudens to produce the Shaw monument, fourteen of the best years of his life. A number of his tentative sketches for this work are preserved. The earlier ones give but little promise of the dignity and beauty of the finished work. We have also numerous notes on his experiences as the work progressed. He got out of them all the fun they had to offer, for fun came home to him without being called. But there was more of work and experiment and self-criticism and taxing of his imagination for a design of greater power and distinction. He set for his standard the saying, "You can do anything you please. It's the way it's done that makes the difference." At another time he declared, "Too much time cannot be spent in a task that is to endure for centuries," and these words appear on the tablet which was erected to his memory a year ago in the Hall of Fame.

The main thing in all this is the glowing ideal of beauty and sublimity that so dominated the spirit of the artist that he was willing to live laborious days and keep at his task even when it reached far out into the years. Every true workman must be a true artist in this. It is here that the aspiration after one's highest possible achievement passes into the moral life of the man, and keeps a pure fire burning in the depths of his soul. It is this undying aspiration that keeps a man working on through temporary and apparent failure, to ends that are durably his own because he believes in them and loves them.

XIII

DECLARATION AND CONSTITUTION

An Address Commemorating the Sesqui-Centennial of the Declaration of Independence, delivered at the Cathedral of St. John the Divine, July 4, 1926

XIII

DECLARATION AND CONSTITUTION

A CENTURY and a half from the signing of the Declaration of Independence, we recall in this service the memory of that historic event. A century from the day when Thomas Jefferson and John Adams passed from earth, we recall their gift to the nation and to mankind. They were brothers in a perilous cause. A temporary estrangement could not divide them. And at the last they answered in unison to one clear trumpet, sounded from afar, in that first jubilee of their patriotic devotion.

They were fathers of revolution. We, in our turn, are sons of revolution. There is revolution in our blood. So much the more important is it that we should read our national history aright.

The Constitution should be read along with the Declaration of Independence. Nothing can dim the historic significance of that earlier document. But without its later companion and complement it might have recorded but one shining hour of freedom, on the way from despotism, through anarchy, back into another despotism. It was the spirit of '89 that saved the fruits of the spirit of '76. The Declaration led the way to liberty; the Constitution secured the blessings of liberty to succeeding generations.

Through years of sharp political experience, through bitter strife that culminated in civil war, America learned at length

A FEW REMARKS

the lesson that liberty alone is not enough, that union is the shield of liberty.

It is one of the whimsical sayings of Maeterlinck that the past is changeable. "Our past," he says, "depends entirely upon our present, and is constantly changing with it." Herein is a notable illustration of that saying. To the end of the Revolution, the Declaration of Independence was a bill of separation, a liberation from an intolerable union. In the course of events it became the first stage of a new union. Even then, its full meaning could not be read till the Civil War had done its work, and our people, North and South, together had entered upon the final task of consummating a more perfect union, the end whereof should be more perfect liberty.

The originals of the Declaration of Independence and the Constitution of the United States have now been committed to the custody of the Librarian of Congress. It is fitting and significant that they are to remain together. They have been placed side by side, in an appropriate depository, where they may be both safe and readily accessible. No careless hand may touch them, but any visitor may see them. Their simple shrine is a center of pilgrimage for American citizens and for visitors from distant lands; and the little children of our schools come there to look upon these parchments, with a rising sense of reverence and responsibility.

I stress the word responsibility. It took our people generations to learn that union, with its obligations, is a necessary support of national liberty. We cannot wonder then that men are slow to learn the more personal lesson, that duty is the major part of freedom. If America is to lead the world into peace, she must learn these lessons in their ultimate meaning. Let her learn, that she may rightly lead. Pray God that she may learn with no more severity of discipline than she

DECLARATION AND CONSTITUTION

has already undergone. But let her even pass under the chastening rod, if the teaching cannot be perfected under the milder mastership of her prosperity.

The Fathers of our Constitution sought to realize liberty and independence by measures which should thereafter render revolutionary violence unnecessary if not impossible. In Europe, after the Napoleonic wars, the Holy Alliance sought by different means to put an end to war and revolution. Their reliance was upon a union of despotic powers, which should forcibly suppress the larger aspirations of their people. The American plan has been that of orderly provision for realizing such aspirations.

Let us not minimize the difficulties which the framers of our Constitution encountered. Independence had brought with it a situation of extraordinary complexity. The work to be done was a work for statesmen. While it was full of emotional and human elements, it was also a problem in the expert adjustment of means to ends, in the discriminating and equalizing of powers, in the distribution of burdens. It called for experience in the processes of government, and a large knowledge of the experience of other governments. It called for coördinating and creative thought. It called for invincible patience. If the statesmen of that time had failed to meet these requirements, the Declaration of Independence might have been lost to the history of human achievement, as another cry of the human spirit, choked and washed away in the deep. But the men of that generation did not fail. Independence became an enduring fact. The Declaration of Independence became one of the living charters of human liberty.

But if the Constitution and government under the Constitution saved the fruits of the Revolution, it was because the spirit of the Constitution was already present in the Revolution itself, latent in the fibre of the makers of the Revolution. They were not lovers and promoters of discontent. They were not "revolutionaires" in the ordinary sense of the word. For them revolution was a last resort, and even then it was a step toward better government.

We come back, then, to the Declaration and the man who framed it. Here was a tall Virginian, unmindful of appearances and of mere conventions, marvellously alert in mind, many-sided in his talents and his interests, well-read in the learning of the ancients and the moderns, and particularly in the liberal utterances of eighteenth-century France and England. One of the youngest members of the Congress, he was nevertheless one of the best equipped to express the sentiments of that body. More revolutionary than many of his associates, he was capable of splendid inconsistency, and was throughout a lover of good government.

The act of separation from the Mother Country had been embodied in the Lee resolution, adopted on the second of July. What remained was to make formal announcement of this act, and to submit "to a candid world" a statement of the facts and considerations which justified its adoption. This announcement and statement of causes had already been prepared in committee, where Jefferson's first draft of the document had not been greatly modified. It was debated at length in the Congress, where again it received only minor amendment. Then finally, on the evening of the fourth of July, it was adopted as "The unanimous Declaration of the thirteen united States of America."

The Declaration interpreted American independence to the world. But more than that, it interpreted American independence to Americans. Out of much confusion, it showed them plainly what they were fighting for. It soon became to

DECLARATION AND CONSTITUTION

them an ensign and a rallying cry. Eventually it became a very ark of their covenant.

Today, it requires no greater stress of thought to pass from the affairs of the nation to affairs of the world than was required in those earlier days to pass from the affairs of the colony to those of an inchoate nation. Many will see an analogy that is rather more than an analogy in the world relationships of the present hour. The tradition of war is a tyranny that even now overshadows the world. But there is a spirit abroad among men which declares against this tyranny. In some form or other must be accomplished, on this world-wide scene, the miracle that was wrought when the American Constitution gave permanent effect to American Independence. Many are now asking whether the statesmanship of this age shall prove equal to the supreme requirement of this age, as the statesmanship of the seventeen-eighties proved equal to the crisis with which that age was confronted.

Let us not be misled by analogies. That would be a childish mistake. A world-wide tyranny can be permanently overcome by world-wide union, and in no other way: that, I think, is unquestionably true. But to unite the nations in an organized world, is a task far different from that of organizing thirteen colonies into a nation. Not only is it greater in magnitude, but it is also different in kind. It involves the coördination of different races. It is concerned with nationalities no longer plastic, schooled in different codes and creeds, overborne by hatreds that are centuries old.

The problem of the twentieth-century world is accordingly different from the problem of eighteenth-century America. Yet the comparison of the two has a value that is not to be ignored. Let us not forget that the men of the eighteenth century were dealing in like manner with new problems, such

A FEW REMARKS

as had never before been solved and had never before been presented. Now as then, the largest wisdom and imagination must combine to produce organs of the public will that can function continuously and effectively, under the hands of men of human passions and human weaknesses. The purpose is supreme; but the mechanism must be such as to serve and not to thwart the purpose. The forces of individual leadership within the mechanism, the intelligence, will, and coöperative capacity of the men who shall direct its several operations—these, at length, will be the determining factors in its success or failure.

No one can question that here is work for the highest statesmanship that any age has produced. But modern statesmen are representatives as well as leaders of public opinion. Their task is conditioned by the choice, the interest, the support of their constituencies. A share of the burden of the world comes back, then, upon the shoulders of every citizen. And that our citizens, the rank and file, shall bear their part of the burden, everywhere throughout the land—this must concern the churches and the schools. Together the churches and the schools must do their part to maintain among our people a conscience and an intelligence that shall match the demands that we make upon our political leaders.

Nowhere is there need for greater wisdom as regards the problem of which I have spoken. There are those who would disparage patriotism in the schools, thinking thereby to promote the interest of internationalism. There are those who would have the churches undermine our most moderate national defense, thinking thereby to make an end to war. We can agree with their aims, some of them, at least, and yet disagree with their proposals.

A weakened America will not serve the ends of world-

DECLARATION AND CONSTITUTION

union or of world peace. Nationalism is still the sentiment from which a wholesome internationalism is to proceed. That we may maintain such nationalism at its best estate, it is fitting that we should pay reverence to the memory of the Fathers and that we should penetrate more deeply into the meaning of their services. We cannot do this with the blind devotion of some part of the nineteenth century. It is to be hoped that we shall not do it in that more modern spirit which seeks for rottenness as the only reality. The men of the Revolution were men of their own age, but they had nevertheless a virtue in them for succeeding ages. They were human in their weaknesses, but they were human also in their strength. I had almost risked the scorn of the sophisticated, to call them more than human in their strength.

Thomas Jefferson's weaknesses are plain to see. But in the totality of his services, how great, how great a man! Most informal in his religion, he yet served the church in truth through his stand for religious liberty. An antifederalist, he nevertheless used the federal power in its widest extent in a national crisis. Trusting the popular will to the verge of idolatry, he labored for the education of the people, in all the grades of education, and crowned his life-work with the establishment of the University of Virginia. A man, in truth, whom we do well to honor, in that remarkable company where Washington was first of all.

But what they did, that glorious company, doth not yet appear, save only in part. It changes with the generations, as its results unfold. It may be that in this generation again it shall prove the seed of unimagined good to all mankind. That depends on the soil as well as the sowing. We may devoutly hope that the America of their making, shall itself make for a new world, a world organized for freedom and for peace.

A FEW REMARKS

To the attainment of such an end we may, all of us, in unison with the Fathers, with a firm reliance on the protection of Divine Providence, mutually pledge to each other our lives, our fortunes, and our sacred honor.

XIV

GUIDE OF LIFE

An Address delivered at the Annual Dinner of Alpha Chapter of Michigan of the Phi Beta Kappa at Ann Arbor, May 5, 1931

XIV

GUIDE OF LIFE

WHEN Emerson delivered his Phi Beta Kappa address on "The American Scholar," nearly a hundred years ago, he alluded to the then recent formation of the British Association for the Advancement of Science. There seems a hint of disparagement in the allusion, slight as it is. Yet he proceeded to call upon "man thinking" to master nature as his own "other me," to master it in both knowledge and action. "So much of nature as he is ignorant of, so much of his own mind he does not yet possess."

What triumphs of physical science and its applications the years had then in store for that generation and those next following! Before Emerson had passed from this earthly scene, in 1882, the physical sciences were advancing to the intellectual conquest of the world, and were laying down their law upon the world of human intelligence. Another decade, and in the eyes of devotees their conquest was complete, and all that remained to be done was a mopping up of particulars, "in the fourth decimal place." But yet another decade had hardly passed when a great change was apparent. Science itself, the science of the twentieth century, had begun to undermine the hasty pretensions of nineteenth-century science. In these more recent years, the accumulation of knowledge of the physical universe has gone forward with accelerated speed, but in the same years new hints, new surmise, new revelation, have entered into the vast undertaking. Now some of the ablest of our scientists, some of those most loyal to the scientific tradition, find themselves driven to philosophizing, and that not only for the mastery of an avalanche of new information, but still more for the mastery of meanings, which new discoveries demand and do not themselves supply. The newer literature in this field is doubtless so well known to all of you that I need not here indulge in bibliography. It is enough to say that physical science and life itself are manifestly laying a new and weighty responsibility upon whatever the philosophical thinking of the age may bring into being, while the old-time opposition between science and the humanities has been softened if not obliterated.

"Philosophy, guide of life," was the motto that had been adopted by our Fraternity, long before Emerson was born. But is philosophy the guide of our life today? There are those who will say *no* in the name of science. There are those who will say *no* in the name of religion. There are those who will say *no* in the name of common sense.

Why may we not discuss that question here this evening? The occasion seems peculiarly fitting. We have begun in a manner altogether in keeping with a long tradition of philosophical intercourse: in other words, we have enjoyed a good dinner, and it has fortified the endurance both of those who have to listen and of those who have to speak. Furthermore, we have followed a newer and distinctively American tradition, in that we have rigorously excluded every extraneous and befuddling spirit, which might otherwise have overstimulated our emotional nature at the expense of sheer, unclouded intellect. We are prepared to pass an unbiased American judgment upon the watchword of this our historic American institution.

To the best of my knowledge, Phi Beta Kappa has never sharply defined its own philosophy. It has never been committed to any philosophical system. It has tacitly approved the paradox that it accepts philosophy for its guide without accepting *a* philosophy. That is a shameless inconsistency, but it may well be that there lies the strength of our position.

The urge that drives a true philosopher to frame a system of philosophy is one of the cleanest and finest to which human nature can respond. It calls for unspeakable toil and effort, for sleepless nights, for alternations of despair and exaltation, for endurance of slights from one's fellow men, and a sense of one's own futility lurking in every dialectic ambush, or perhaps a hardening of one's mind in the confidence that no other undertaking in all the world can offer such ultimate reward, such uncorrupted value for all mankind. It is the far call which has summoned so many of the highest spirits in human history to a supreme endeavor, the endeavor to round out at length all fragmentary conceptions of the universe and of human destiny into a complete circle of indubitable knowledge.

But after all the high endeavor of the loftiest minds down through the ages, the circle will not hold; its passing semblance of completeness fades away. It is as if each irrefragable doctor in his turn, lured by the happy beginnings of a rounded system, had been convinced that the finished circle was within his reach, had shaped it, provisionally at least, with some straining of his definitions—into the perfection of that circle; and yet those coming after him have found reality breaking here and there through the lines of his design, and opening up again the old, old question of ultimate truth.

Let me carry the geometric metaphor a little farther: it may dawn upon us at last that the form of our knowledge is not that of a circle but that of a parabola. We think it is about to come round into the finished and final circumference, but every effort to reach that consummation does violence, sooner or later,

A FEW REMARKS

to larger revelations of truth that are awaiting us. The farther we advance into the unknown the farther away seems that completeness for which we had hoped and striven. Seeking a circle, self-contained and absolute, we have drawn this vast parabola of thought farther and farther out upon the unbounded deep, and have widened out more and more the shadowy apprehension of things unknown.

I hope my fanciful, Euclidean figure may not obscure the thought it is meant to illustrate. It may well be that our modes of thought, inevitably adjusted to a mode of existence in which we have five senses only to bring us information of the sensible world—or six senses or eight or nine as the psychologists may decide—and these shaping for us a world of only three dimensions, regardless of what the mathematicians may say: it may be that our modes of thought somehow related to such conditions can never find for us the answer to the larger questions which the human mind avails to ask. It may be that the ultimate answers, if such ultimate there be, can be had only in an existence other than that which we have for a moment or two upon this earth. But whatever the explanation, thus far we find the unknown widening out, instead of narrowing down, with every advance into that realm of the unexplored. Nevertheless, that fact can in no way abate the ardor of the exploration. And the service of the explorers—scientists and philosophers, whether the two be different or identical—is not to be measured by their power to say the final word.

Systems come and systems go in the history of philosophical speculation, but none of them comes and goes in vain. Each system leaves its deposit of reasoned ideas to enrich the thought that shall come after. In particular, each one sets up here and there in its turn the warning sign, *No thoroughfare*, and this of itself is a lasting gain.

GUIDE OF LIFE

In that decade of the eighteen-hundred-thirties, Hegelianism was well-nigh a governmental establishment of philosophy in the German universities. In the eighteen-hundred-eighties its reign was over in Germany, at the very time that it was having a belated and transient revival in the British Isles, and a considerable vogue here in America. At the same time Spencerianism was winning its wide following, a following sometimes animated with sheer fanatical devotion. Pragmatism followed after, having its definite rise and an indefinite spread of influence, as it developed in a variety of forms. How many other philosophic modes and trends in this past seething century of ideas, who now would undertake to say? No one of these major currents has simply led mankind astray. All have entered into the thought of our time, all have helped in the thinking that our modern world must do.

For, while we recognize the futility of any attempt to crystallize philosophic speculation into an unalterable system, final and complete, the old paradox is with us yet. We have still the insistent demand, the intensified need, of philosophic thinking. We invoke such thought to rescue us from worse than chaos, in a world that is deluged with new knowledge. The world of action requires it, universities are painfully aware of the need, individuals everywhere are facing crises which demand reasoned and reasonable choices and decisions.

What, then, is philosophic thinking *sans* a philosophy? In those bald terms, the question is unfair, for see how the two are interwoven: *A* philosophy is ordinarily the work of an individual. It is the philosophy of Plato, of Thomas Aquinas, of Spinoza, of Kant, Hegel, Spencer, Wundt. Even so, it does not stand alone, but gathers into itself, for acceptance, criticism, or rejection, the work of its predecessors. It is one man's philosophy because he has fashioned it and made it his own. It is not

A FEW REMARKS

the philosophy of any other, not even of his disciples, unless by their own free thought they have made his thought their own. It is not a commodity or a legacy that can be simply passed from one to another. No man has a philosophy save as he has thought it out for himself. Every man has a philosophy to the extent that he has done philosophic thinking on his own account. And every philosophy, great or small, if it be sincere, will seek with steadfast purpose for the complete answer and explanation, for some semblance of the rounded circle.

So the question comes again, what is philosophic thinking? I will not attempt a definition, but I may offer a few suggestions. Philosophic thinking, whether that of the philosopher or that of the man in the street, has its background in the best thought of mankind. That is its prime condition. In the thought of the ripened philosopher, the background is the long history of systematic philosophy and systematic theology, twin sciences if not Siamese twins. If his thinking is broad enough, the background will be nothing less than our historic civilization. Even those who are not philosophers by profession or by specialization will find their thought, as it advances, rising to heights of appreciation of the great thinkers of the past and more and more influenced by the masterpieces of their genius. Philosophic thinking, whether that of the professional philosopher or of the layman, will in increasing measure find materials for its thought in other masterpieces, notably those of the poets and the writers of fiction, for some of the more subtle problems of thought are to be taken by flank movements rather than by direct assault.

Two of the elements of creative thinking have been in a measure overlooked by the greatest of systematizers; namely, the element of beauty and that of humor. What might not Aristotle have done for the world if he could have added the

GUIDE OF LIFE

art of Plato to his supreme dialectic! And what might have happened to Hegel if he could have had some little touch of Shakespeare's comedy! The philosophic thought of men who are not primarily philosophers will draw heavily upon the larger literatures of the world, from Homer to Chaucer and all the way down to Mark Twain and Bernard Shaw. From them it will acquire, according to individual powers of assimilation, some measure of that balance, poise, urbanity, discrimination, which we all attribute to a philosophic spirit.

Philosophic thinking, if it be soundly philosophic, will face courageously the facts of nature and man as it finds them; but it will just as courageously refuse to take surface appearances as final and will probe for underlying causes, forces, principles, meanings. To this end, it will shun hasty conclusions, and will wait for what second thought, or a thought beyond, or sustained inquiry, may reveal. It will, on occasion, sacrifice momentary efficiency to remoter achievement.

Philosophic thinking aims at logical consistency and is inhospitable to patent contradictions. It may make much or little deliberate use of the historic forms of logic. It will as it matures become aware of the fact that meticulous consistency tends to obscure the larger truth. But however much it may prize the hints and leads of artistic imagination, it will not readily accept a happy surmise for proof, where reasoned insight is attainable.

Philosophic thinking will not be unmindful of historic and institutionalized faiths and loyalties, but it will hold these subject to independent scrutiny, as regards both their superficial aspect and their deeper significance. Such thinking will free itself equally from traditional prejudice, from current shibboleths, and from the sudden stampede of the mob. It will accept personal responsibility for individual opinions, well knowing that pride of opinion has dangers of its own and that the long judgment of mankind is often wiser than the hasty convictions of any man. It will at least gain sufficient detachment to form judgments untainted by self-seeking, and will realize that self-seeking has its more subtle and bewildering forms, as well as the grosser and more obvious, and that these may well deceive the very elect.

Philosophic thinking will find place for the long thoughts which mature in solitude. If actual solitude is unattainable, it will learn to make on occasion a solitude of its own in the midst of the crowd and the day's work. But it will be aware that thinking is not all of life nor even the greater bulk of life, which is made up of action, work, strife, adventure, art, sport, sheer human intercourse, love, religion, the interweaving of life and death. In all of these, nevertheless, it will participate, never renouncing its dignity and function as seeker after truth and reasonableness. In both prosperity and adversity it will moderate emotional excess. In the strife of parties it will seek for higher levels on which honest men may come together. In the mysticism which may arise in solitude, it will curb the tendency to visionary extravagance and fanaticism.

Philosophic thinking seeks inevitably for unity of some sort in the whirl and clatter of diversity. It may be misled into accepting unsubstantial unities. They have undoubtedly been assumed too easily by serious seekers after truth, even by the very makers of great historic systems of philosophy. But I cannot believe that because accepted unities may have been found wanting, any genuine philosophic thinking in this or any other age will take whirl as its lord and king, or admit that the end of all its seeking is chaos.

Something of this our Fraternity stands for. In some such sense as this it holds philosophy to be the guide of life. Not of an unthinking, however forceful and achieving life; but of a life worthy of a thinking man or woman, a life that may have in it something of austerity and sacrifice for the present moment, but looks to the larger good of the longer day. Such is the purpose that we lay before the more gifted undergraduates in our colleges, and there is never a lack of those for whom it has its appeal. Some of the best work in our national history has been done by such as these. Some of the best work of the future they will do, and that in larger measure than in the past.

But in a time when so much of confusion spreads through all our life—our academic as well as our artistic, religious, and ethical life—it becomes necessary for us to consider in a larger way the need of philosophic thought in our universities. Let us give some consideration to this topic.

University teachers in these days are learners as well as teachers, and their aim in teaching is not to make students learned but to make them learners, like themselves. That is taken for granted. The most of these teachers are themselves researchers as well as learners. They expect to make some contribution of their own to the stock of human knowledge. Some of them, a smaller number, recognize the further fact that their several subjects can never be complete in themselves, but must find a large measure of their truth in their relations with other subjects; and if they take this fact in its full significance, they know that none of their several subjects can be really true save as it finds its place in the whole range of truth, that their thought upon any specialty is inadequate unless it rise to the level of philosophic thinking. Still further, their thought upon any subject, however abstruse or material, cannot be regarded as at its best unless it take account of human relationships, in the endeavor to see the bearing of their teaching and research upon the whole round of human life.

A FEW REMARKS

All of this the world has a right to expect of its universities. It is too much to expect of every teacher in a university, particularly of our younger instructors. The most immature among them, however, should have some inkling of the wider relationships of that which he is teaching, and until he is able to look a little way beyond the lessons of today and the researches of today, he is not rightly prepared for a university position. Let us go farther and say that no department of university teaching—or closely connected group of departments—can be regarded as adequately organized unless there be within it at least one teacher who gives competent and continued study to the relationships of those subjects to the wider range of knowledge and of education. Such study necessarily includes an historic as well as a philosophic approach. We may go still one step farther, and ask of every university that it have one or more members who look forth serenely upon the whole passing show of human affairs, as wise interpreters and prophets of the better life of mankind. The philosophic thinking abroad in every rightly constituted university should rise to some such mountainous culmination.

Let me play a bit with this idea before I close, for it seems to me one that may profitably be considered—seriously but not too seriously. I should not think of proposing the formal designation of a nestor or a panel of nestors for any university. That would be an occasion for academic mirth. Besides no man would be fit for such designation if he lacked the sense of humor which would prompt him to share on his own account in such derision. But while the formal office is impossible its equivalent is indispensable. The founders of New York University declared a century ago, that "the legitimate object of a university is not only the education of youth, but the fuller development of the minds of men." That statement will indi-

GUIDE OF LIFE

cate what I have in mind: the consummate teacher of men; the ripe scholar and masterly thinker to whom men will resort, even at the height of their career, for stimulus and illumination. So Bishop Berkeley at Newport two centuries ago alternated between solitary meditation and enlivening intercourse with influential Colonials of that time; so Thomas Jefferson was himself a university for men at Monticello before his university for younger men came into being at Charlottesville; so professors of biology gathered around Agassiz at Penikese Island; so Valentine Mott and other great surgeons and physicians taught and led their fellow professionals, as others are doing down to the present day; so college teachers once turned to the Concord summer school of philosophy; so Whitney at Yale and Gildersleeve at Johns Hopkins drew our American philologists into their circle of light; so William T. Harris was chief consultant of educational leaders throughout the land. In the broad outlook over human affairs, perhaps our chief example in recent times was President Eliot of Harvard. Happy is the institution that finds such a man in its membership and gives him opportunity, as his powers ripen and his influence widens, to do this highest work of a university.

The particular reason for laying emphasis here on such superprofessorial activities in university life, is the need of philosophic thinking in its maturest living forms today, in view of the unprecedented influx of new knowledge, new experience, new intellectual, economic, governmental, and spiritual adventure. It would seem incumbent upon our oldest of American fraternities to exercise its influence in our American universities to the end that philosophic thinking, up into the highest ranges of teaching and research, far beyond that leading to any academic degree, shall guide American life into the finest and most substantial achievement of which it is humanly capable.

This would mean that universities should be concerned not only with the teaching of students and the teaching of teachers, but with the teaching of the teachers of teachers of teachers, up to the highest significance of that expression. The problems of society tend more and more to become problems of education, and the great problem of education is the problem of the kind of society we wish our education to create and re-create. This is a problem not for mere pedagogues, but for men, and men in all of the higher ranges of our life. I seem to foresee the development in our universities of such spiritual leadership as shall arrest the attention and further the explorations of those men and women, in whatever walk of life, who shall take the most responsible and farsighted and creative view of our life as a whole, national and international—who shall competently make philosophy the guide of life for our America and for our human world.

INDEX

INDEX

Academy of Medicine of Northern New Jersey, address before. *See* Scientist and Artist
Adams, Henry, 86
Adams, James Truslow, 87
Adams, John, 40, 217
Adult education, 106
Advancing South, The 186
Agassiz, Jean Louis R., 237
Aims of Education, The, 122
Aleut, education of the, 13
Alexander, George, v
Allegiances, problem of, 180
Ambrogio, Traversari, 75
American Architecture, 86 n.
American Architecture of Today, The, 86 n.
American Expeditionary Force, 163
American Government. *See* Declaration and Constitution
American Institute of Architects, 87
American Philosophical Society, 98
American Revolution, Sons of the, 104
American Society of Newspaper Editors, 177
Amherst College, 103
Anarchy, 137
Angell, President James B., 11, 57
Annual Reports of the Chancellor of New York University. *See under* Democracy and Democratic Education; Numbers, A Book of; Imagination and Memory; Urbanity, On; Beauty and the University
Antæus, 151
Aquinas, Thomas, 231
Architectural Institute of America, 211
Architecture, 85, 86
Aristotle, 54, 120, 232
Army Mental Tests, 44
Arnold, Matthew, 33, 107, 111
Art, The Meaning of, 127 n.
Art, relationship to morals, 131
Art and the Reformation, 87
Artist Mechanics, 205–213:
    The artist in the workman, two examples of, 207–208; an example of the creative instinct of the artist in everyday business, 209–210; importance of learning the rules of the craft first, 211; methods of Saint Gaudens in perfecting his work, 212–213
Artist and physician, 161. *See* Chapters VIII and XII *passim*
Association, British, for the Advancement of Science, 227
Astoria, Ill., 6
Auerbach, Joseph S., 81 & n.

Baccalaureate Address by the Chancellor of New York University. *See under* One and All; Duty of Thinking, The
Bacon, Henry, 85
Bagley, W. C., 198
Bain, Professor Alexander, 199
Baker, Professor George Pierce, 108
Baker, Professor Franklin T., 197
Balboa, 148
Baldwin, Professor Elizabeth G., 197
Barnard, President Frederick A. P., 195
Barzizza, Gasparino, 75
Beauty and the University, 115–133:
    Vitality of beauty in life, 115; inclusion of the arts in Greek education, 118; the mediaeval university's primary concern was with truth, 119; beauty introduced by Renaissance Humanists into education, 120; the post-Renaissance return to scholasticism and study of the classics, 121; Hegel and nineteenth-century education, 123; modern shift in emphasis from defense of truth to its scientific ascertainment, 124; present cry for self-expression likely to cause a renaissance of beauty, 125; necessity of a more adequate system of teaching in aesthetic fields, 126; the rebel artist personality and need for the elevation of taste, 127; the university teaching of beauty becomes as important as truth, 129; the close relationship of art and morals, 131

A FEW REMARKS

Belvidere, Ill., 6
Bénard, M. E., 211
Berkeley, Bishop George, 237
Berlin, 94
Bibliography, partial, of Chancellor Brown's educational writings, 9–11
Bigelow, Maurice A., 197
Board of Education, English, 40
Bohr, N. H. D., 77
Book of Numbers, A. See Numbers, A Book of
Bookman, The, 105
Boston, Mass.: State House, 212; Common, 212; Shaw monument, 212
Boyce Thompson Institute for Plant Research, 98
Brevoort, Henry, 137
Bridges, Robert, 128
British Association for the Advancement of Science, 227
Brown, Chancellor Elmer Ellsworth: Annual Reports, see Chapters I–V; Baccalaureate Addresses, see Chapters IX and X; partial bibliography of the works of, 9–11; his birth, 5; his family moves to Illinois, 5; graduated from Illinois State Normal School, 6; high-school principal at Astoria, Ill., 6; superintendent of schools at Belvidere, Ill., 6; organizes Northern Illinois Teachers' Association, 6; becomes State Secretary of Illinois Y.M.C.A., 6; freshman at University of Michigan, 5, 6; graduated from University of Michigan, 6; marriage, 6; graduate study in Germany, 7; high-school principal of Jackson, Mich., 7; acting assistant professor, University of Michigan, 7; organizes department of Education, University of California, 7; heads National Bureau of Education, 9, 11, 12–14; accepts Chancellorship of New York University, 11, 14, 15; publications of, 3, 7; see also partial bibliography, 9–11; tribute to, by Professor Gayley, 8; correspondence of, 11; hospitality of, 3; character of, 8, 9; as a speaker, 8; home at University Heights, 3, 4, 15; Professor Miller's short biography of, 4–8
Brown, Fanny Eddy, 6, 15
Brown, I. E., 6
Bryan, William Jennings, 187
Bryce, James, 11
Bulletin of the Metropolitan Museum, New York City, 127 n.
Burdon, Richard, Viscount Haldane, 33
Bureau of the Census, 13
Bureau of Education, 12
Burnham, Daniel, 85
"Business Conduct, Principles of," 177
Business, growth towards a professional status, 176
Busse, Alvin C., 63
Butler, President Nicholas Murray, 11, 196–197

CALIFORNIA, University of, 7, 78, 211
Cambridge University, 118, 119, 122
Canfield, President James Hulme, 9
Canons of Journalism, 177
Carnegie Foundation, 46
Cathedral of St. John the Divine, 214
Catherine, Empress of Russia, 20
Causabon, Isaac, 120
Census, Bureau of the, 13
Chamber of Commerce of the U. S., 177
Charlottesville, Va., 237
Charters, Professor W. W., 56
Chaucer, Geoffrey, 233
Cheney, Howell, 46
Chicago, Ill., 94, 117
Chicago, University of, 56, 58
Chinese writers, 191
Christianity, 138, 142
Ciceronian Tradition, 76, 122
City Committee on Plan and Survey, 94
City School Systems, 199
City school systems and the urban university, 95
Civil War, 181, 189
Clark University Press, 43 n.
"Classical Tradition in Poetry, The," 131
Clemens, S. L. ("Mark Twain"), 233
Cleveland, O., 94

INDEX

Cobb, Henry I., 85
Coleridge, Samuel T., 87
Colet, John, 75
College Education, Problems of, 55
Colleges, U. S.: Amherst, Haverford, Knox, Randolph-Macon, Vassar, 103
Colonial Dames, 104
Columbia University, 197. *See under* Teachers College
Commerce, Chamber of, of the U. S., 177
Committee, City, on Plan and Survey, 94
Commissioner of Education, 5
Committee of Ten, Report of the, 200
Compayré, Gabriel, *The History of Pedagogy,* translated by W. H. Payne, 199
Concord Summer School of Philosophy, 237
Conservatism, 186
Constitution, U. S., 217
Cook, John W., 11
Coolidge, President Calvin, 175
Cooper, Professor Lane, 87
Cope, Walter, 85
Cornell, Ezra, 100
Cornell University, 87
Coulton, G. C., 87
Cram, Ralph Adams, 85
Creative Power, 79
Creative Youth, 79
Curie, Mme. Marie, 77
Cyclopedia of Education, 201

Daniel Guggenheim School of Aeronautics, 159
Dante, 191
Darrow, Clarence, 187
Dartmouth College, 55
Darwin, Charles, 129
Day, Frank M., 85
Dayton, Tenn., 187
Dean Russell's Quarter Century. *See under* Russell
Declaration and Constitution, 215-224: Importance of studying the Declaration of Independence along with the Constitution, 217; obligations of liberty not to be lost sight of in the desire for the privileges that it confers, 218; difficulties in framing the Constitution, 219; importance of the Declaration of Independence as an interpreter to America of its ideals, 220; present-day need of similar intelligence for the settling of modern world-problems, 221; the resultant burden of coöperation upon the citizens, 222; nationalism the best tool with which to secure healthy internationalism, 223; the desired rôle of America in world freedom and peace, 223-224
Declaration of Independence, 217
Defoe, Daniel, 104
Delano, William A., 85
Democracy, essentials for, 137, 139; imagination essence of, 80
Democracy and Democratic Education, 17-34: Democracy based on personality, 19; each man leader and led, 21; demand for equal opportunity in education, 22; opposing groups of conservatism and demagogy, 24; a society of human organizations, 25; education for group-life, 26; training of artisan and man, 27; the individual and institutions, 28; humanistic and scientific aspects, 29; education the concern of the state, 29; citizenship of the world, 30; the religious element in democracy, 32; democracy of universities, 32
Dewey, Professor John, 79, 198
Dialectic, 120, 121, 188
Diana, Saint Gauden's statue of, 212
Diderot, Denis, 20
Dissenters, 104
Division of Educational Reference established at Purdue, 56
Division of Higher Education, 56
Dodge, Professor Richard E., 197
D'Ooge, Martin L., 11
Draper, A. S., 11
Durand, John, 31 n.
Durham, Jim, 209
Dutton, Professor Samuel Train, 198; life of, 198

A FEW REMARKS

Duty of Thinking, The. *See under* Thinking, The Duty of

Ecclesiasticus, quotation from, 165
École des Beaux Arts, 86
Eddy, Fanny, 6, 15
Eddy, Dr. Zachary, 6
Edgell, G. H., 86 n.
Education: adult, 106; Aleut, 13; equal opportunity for, 22; freer election of studies, 78; early literature on, 195; future humanistic, 139; a concern of the state, 29; rôle in group-life, 26; Greek, 118; heredity in, 43; American instruction in, 195; individual capacity for, 42; moral stamina demanded, 50; moral values of, 51; in the Renaissance, 53; social sympathies of the individual enlarged by, 181
Education, The Aims of, 122
Education Board, General, 46
Education, U. S. Bureau of, 12
Education, Commissioner of, 5
Education, Cyclopaedia of, by Paul Monroe, 201
Education, English Board of, 40
Education, Federal Office of, 37, 56
Education, Higher, Journal of, 56
Education, History of, by Paul Monroe, 201
Education, National Bureau of, 9
Education, National Council of, 7
Educational Reformers, Quick's *Essays on,* 199
"Education, The Rhythm of," 122
Education, School of, New York University, 59, 202
Education as a Science, 199
Educational Association, National, 12
Educational Reference, Division of, 56
Einstein, Albert, 77
Eliot, President Charles W., 50, 77, 237
Elliott, President Edward C., 56
Elliott, Professor W. Y., 33
Emerson, Ralph Waldo, 33, 147, 227, 228
Engineering, 174, 175
English Board of Education, 40
Enrollment, recent increase in, 37

Erasmus, Desiderius, 74, 75
Erasmus, Desiderius, 74
Eskimo, 13
Essays and Miscellanies, 81
Evolution, The Limits of, 54 & n.
Exchange of Letters, An, 60–69
Experimental Psychology, The Foundations of, 43

Facilities for *Study and Research in Washington, D. C.,* 12
Fame, Hall of, 213
Fanny Eddy Brown Collection of Modern Verse, 15
Farragut, David G., statue of, 181, 212
Federal Office of Education, 37, 56
da Feltre, Vittorino, 74
Ferry Building, San Francisco, 211
Fisher, Herbert A. L., 40–42
Florence, 159
Foundations of Experimental Psychology, The, 43
France, 30
Frank, President Glenn, 190
Freedom and Discipline, The Rhythmic Claims of, 122
Freeman, Kenneth J., 118–119
Froebel, Friedrich W. A., 200
Furst, Clyde, 197

Gallaudet, Thomas, 195
Gary, Judge, 100
Gayley, Professor Charles Mills, 8, 14, 126
Gaza, Theodore, 75
General Education Board, 46
General Society of Mechanics and Tradesmen, address to. *See* Artist Mechanics
General Theological Seminary, 142; address to, *see* Humanistic Studies
George of Trebizond, 75
German Higher Schools, 201
Germany, 7, 231
Gifted students, 49
Gilbert, Cass, 85
Gildersleeve, Professor Basil L., 126, 237
Gonzagas, 75
Goodhue, Bertram G., 85

INDEX

Gorgas, William Crawford, 163
Government by Influence, 53
Grammarian's Funeral, 76
Gray, Dean William S., 56 n.
Great Britain, 67
Greco-Roman culture, 119
Greek, 75
Greeks, 118, 121, 179
Guarino, Battista, 75
Guggenheim, Daniel, School of Aeronautics, 159
Guide of Life, 225–238:
  Demands made by the advances of physical science upon philosophy, 228; possibility of accepting philosophy as a guide without subscribing to *a* philosophy, 229; excessive toil demanded for framing a system of philosophy, 229; failure of any philosophy to reach ultimate truth, 229; the ascendancy of Hegelianism, Spencerism, and Pragmatism, and their permanent contributions to present-day thought, 231; the personal philosophy, 231; philosophic thinking defined: searches for underlying causes, aims at logical consistency, tests historic and institutionalized faiths and loyalties, sets a proper value on occasional solitude, searches for unity, 232–234; how the Phi Beta Kappa Fraternity holds philosophy as its guide to life, 234; necessity of university teachers' appreciating the relation of their subject to others, and its ultimate place in truth, 235; importance of a teacher affiliated with the university who is qualified to guide mature men at the height of their careers in the steps of philosophy, 237
Gummere, Professor Francis B., 126

Hadley, President Arthur Twining, 12
Haldane Commission, 34
Haldane, Viscount, 33–34
Hale, Edward Everett, 11
Hall, President G. Stanley, 200
Hall of Fame, 213

Halle, University of, 7
Harkness, Edward S., 108
Harris, Dr. William T., 123, 200, 237
Harvard University, 33, 77, 78, 122, 237
Hastings, Thomas, 85
Havana, 163
Haverford College, 103
Hearst, Mrs. Phebe A., 211
Hebrew Scriptures, 191
Hegel, Georg W. F., 123, 231, 233
Hegelianism, 231
Hellas, Schools of, 118
Hendrick, Burton, 149
Higher Education, Division of, 56
Higher Education, Journal of, 56
Higher Education, Specialist in, 112
Higher Education, Studies in, 56
Hillegas, Milo, 198
Hinsdale, Professor B. A., 195
History, 139, 142
History of Education, 199
History of the Italian Republics, 141
Hitchcock, E. A., 11
Holmes, Mr. Justice Oliver Wendell, 81 & n.
Holy Alliance, 219
Homer, 191, 233
Hoover, President Herbert Clark, 101
Hopkins, President Mark, 55
"How to make our Ideas Clear," 78
Howard, John Galen, 85, 211
Howells, John Mead, 85
Howison, Professor George Holmes, 54, 78, 123
Hudelson, Earl, 55
Humanistic Studies—A Forecast, 135–143:
  Conflict between Democracy and present-day anarchy, 137; the essentials for a democracy; like-mindedness, coöperation, leaders *en rapport* with the people, considerations of our economic life, 137–139; the consequent future of our education to be humanistic, 139; inevitable interrelationship of science with the humanities, 140; stabilizing virtue of the study of history and its likewise new revelations, 142

245

Hunt, Richard M., 85
Huxley, Thomas, 39

IDEA *of a University, The*, 99
Illinois, University of, 147
Illinois State Normal University, 6
Imagination and Memory, 71–89:
   Present-day shifting of emphasis from memory to imagination, 73; Vittorino da Feltre and Renaissance education, 74; the effect of science and invention in the nineteenth century, 76; innovation of freer election of studies, 78; the effect of pragmatism on education, 79; imagination as the essence of democracy, 80; imagination's dependence on the materials of experience, 81; rôle of memory in disciplining the imagination, 82; memory an indispensable agent in discipline, 83; imagination and memory as sources of criticism, 84; example of disciplined imagination in the case of architecture, 85; imagination in scholarship, 86; imagination in religion, 88; hope of sustaining the present free range of imagination in the University, 89
Independence, Declaration of, 215–224
Indian, American, education of, 13
Indian writers, 191
Industrial Conference Board, National, 56, 216
Industry and the urban university, 199
Influence of Academies, The Literary, 101
Influence, Government by, 53
Institute of Architects, American, 87
Institute of American Meat Packers, 58
Internationalism, 223
Irving, Washington, 137
Isaac Causabon, 1559–1614, 120
Italian Republics, History of, 141
Ivins, William M., 127 n.

JACKSON, Mich., 7
Jackson, Stonewall, 181
James, William, 78, 79
Jefferson, Thomas, 33, 217, 220, 223, 237

Jenney, William L., 85
John, Bishop of Aleria, 75
Johns Hopkins University, 237
Johnston, Professor, W. H., 100
Journal of the Medical Society of New Jersey, 155
Journal of Higher Education, 56
Journalism, Canons of, 177
Journalism as a profession, 177
Justinich, Martin, 3

KANT, Immanuel, 171, 231
Keats, John, 118
Kiantone, N. Y., 5
Kilpatrick, Professor William H., 198
Kimball, Fiske, 86 n.
Kimball, LeRoy Elwood, iii, 3–15
Kipling, Rudyard, 52
Knickerbocker History of New York, 137
Knox College, 103

LA FARGE, John, 212
Lane, Franklin K., 11
Last Supper, 160
Lay Morals, 56
Latin, 75
Lead Kindly Light, 188
Lee resolution, 220
Lee, Robert E., 181
Legal profession, 172
Letters from a Self-made Merchant to his Son, 209
Levermore, Charles Herbert, 198
Leviticus, 180
Library of Congress, 13, 218
Life of Solitude, 147
Life and Letters of Walter H. Page, 149
Lily, William, 76
Limits of Evolution, The, 54 & n.
Lippmann, Walter, 43
Literary Influence of Academies, The, 107
Liverpool, University of, 74
Lodge, Professor Gonzales, 197
Loeb, William, Jr., 11
Logic, 187, 188
London, University of, 34, 122
Lorimer, George Horace, 209
Lowell Foundation, 40

INDEX

Lowes, Professor John L., 86–87

MacDonald, Ramsay, 41
McKim, Charles Follen, 85
McMahon, Professor A. Philip, 127 n.
McMurry, Frank M., 197
Madison Square Garden, 212
Maeterlinck, Maurice, 218
Making of our Middle Schools, The, 7
Mantua, 74
Markham, Edwin, 11
"Martin." *See* Justinich
Marxianism, 80
Materialism, 112
Meaning of Art, The, 127 n.
Mearns, Professor Hughes, 79
Meat Packers, American, Institute of, 58
Mechanism and Laws of Heredity, The, 43
Medical Society of New Jersey, *Journal* of the, 155
Medicine, Academy of, of Northern New Jersey. *See* Scientist and Artist
Medicine and science, 164
Memory, eclipsed today by imagination, 73; value in disciplining imagination, 75
Message from the U. S. Bureau of Education, A, 12
Messiah of Pope, quoted, 39
Meteorology, 97
Metropolitan Museum, *Bulletin* of, 127 n.
Michigan, University of, 5–7, 195
Mill, John Stuart, 67
Millay, Edna St. Vincent, 131
Miller, Governor Nathan, 100
Miller, Professor Walter, 4, 5, 11, 14
Millikan, Robert A., 100
Milton, John, 33, 191
Mims, Professor Edwin, 186–187
Ministry as a profession, 178
Minnesota, University of, 55
Missouri, University of, 5
Modern Regime, The, 30, 31 & n.
Mona Lisa, 160
Monroe, Professor Paul, 198, 201
Monticello, 237
Mont-Saint-Michel and Chartres, 86

Morals, Relation to Art, 131
More, Sir Thomas, 75
Morgan, Professor T. H., 43
Morris, George S., 123
Mott, Valentine, 237
Municipal bureaus and the university, 110
Murchison, Professor Carl, 43
Murray, Professor Gilbert, 130
Music, 118, 120, 121
Mysticism, 88

Napoleon, 30
Napoleonic Wars, 219
Nation, The, 8
National Bureau of Education, 9
National Council of Education, 7
National Educational Association, 7, 12
National Industrial Conference Board, 46, 58
Nationalism, 223
New College, Oxford, 40
Newman, Cardinal John Henry, 33, 99, 188
Newport, 237
New Republic, The, 43
Newspaper Editors, American Society of, 177
"New Tastes in Old Prints," 127 n.
New Willard Hotel, 207
New York City, 39, 91, 94–114, 137, 187, 207
New York State, 39
New York, Knickerbocker History of, 137
New York University, 14, 19, 37, 58, 59, 73, 113, 159, 195, 202, 236
Noble State Bank vs. Haskell, 81 & n.
Normal, Ill., 6
North American Review, The, 44
North Carolina, University of, 4
Northern Illinois Teachers' Association, 6
Norton, Professor Charles Eliot, 126
Numbers, A Book of, 35–59:
Increase in college and high-school enrollments, 37; Huxley's educational ladder, 39; MacDonald's education highway, 41; the individual's capacity for education, 42; heredity

247

A FEW REMARKS

versus education, 43; army mental tests and college enrollment, 44; possible saturation of industries and professions with college-trained persons, 45; waste of maladjustment, 48; vocational guidance, 48; education of gifted students, 49; normal stamina requisite in higher education, 50; higher education should make higher demands, 50; moral values of college education, 51; government by influence, 53; responsibility of instructors to revise their teaching in keeping with the changes in the world, 55; higher education in relation to the general welfare, 56; industry attacks similar problem, 58; New York University's effort, 59

Nutting, Professor Adelaide, 198

OHIO State University, 56
On Urbanity. *See under* Urbanity
One and All, 167–182:
  The good of one to be gained through the good of all, 169; excesses today in the search for beauty in literature and the arts, 170; value of the true scientific spirit to one's personality: in astronomy, law, medicine, engineering, 171–175; definition of a profession, 175; growth of business towards a professional status, 176; of journalism, 177; the profession of the ministry, 178; the fine arts, 179; necessity for concentrating on allegiances, 180; enlargement of one's social sympathies through education, 181

Origin and Antiquity of Man, Recent Discoveries relating to the, 98
Osborn, Henry Fairfield, 98
Ovid, 76

PAGE, Walter H., 149–150; *Life and Letters of,* 149
Panama, 163
Parable of the Good Samaritan, 180
Paris, 94, 141, 211

Paris, University of, 113–114
Paris Exposition, 1900, 7
Pasteur, Louis, 29
Patriotism, 30
Pattison, Mark, 120
Payne, Professor William H., 195, 199
Pedagogy, History of, by Compayré, 199
Pedagogy, School of, New York University, 195
Peirce, Charles, 78
Penikese Island, Buzzard's Bay, 237
Pestalozzi, Johann H., 200
Petrarch, 147, 153
Phi Beta Kappa address of Emerson, 227
Phi Beta Kappa Fraternity, address to, 225–238
Philbrick, John D., 199
Philosophical Society, American, 98
Philosophy: demands of physical science upon, 228; excessive toil demanded for framing a system of, 229; failure to reach ultimate truth, 229; personal philosophy, 231
Philosophy, Concord Summer School of, 237
Pilate, 118
Plan and Survey, City Committee on, 94
Plan d'une université, 20
Plato, 33, 191, 231, 233
Political Economy, Principles of, 67
Politics, 109
Pope, Alexander, his *Messiah* quoted, 39
Popular Science Monthly, 78, 129
Post, William S., 85
Pragmatic Revolt in Politics, 33
Pragmatism, 79, 231
Pragmatism, 78
"Principles of Business Conduct," 177
Principles of Political Economy, 67
"Prints, New Tastes in Old," 127 n.
Problems of College Education, 55
Professional schools, 171–177
Provincial spirit, 107
Psalms, quoted, 151, 171
Psychologic Foundations of Education, 200

INDEX

Psychology, The Foundations of Experimental, 43
Public Education as Affecting the Adjustment of Youth to Life, 46
Publications of the Modern Language Association, 87 n.
Purdue University, 56
Puritanism, 187

Quick, Robert Hebert, 199
Quintilian, 119

Radicalism, 186
Randolph-Macon, 103
Recent Discoveries relating to the Origin and Antiquity of Man, 98
Reformation, Art and the, 87
Reminiscences of Augustus Saint-Gaudens, 212
Renaissance, 89, 120, 121, 159
Report of the Committee of Ten on Secondary School Studies, 200
Reports, Annual, of the Chancellor of New York University. *See under* Annual Reports, Chapters I–V
Revolution, American. *See* Chapter XIII
"Rhythm of Education, The," 122
"Rhythmic Claims of Freedom and Discipline, The," 122
Richardson, Henry H., 85
Road to Xanadu, The, 86–87
Roentgen, Wilhelm H., 77
Rogers, James G., 85
Rome, 110, 120, 141
Roosevelt, President Theodore, 11
Root, John W., 85
Russell, Dean James E. *See* Dean Russell's Quarter-Century, 193–203: Origin of university instruction in education in the United States, 195; foundation of Teachers College, 196; Dean Russell's faculty, 197; Dean Russell as an administrator, 198; educational literature available to American students in 1892, 199; subsequent contributions to educational literature, by Dean Russell's faculty, 200; Dean Russell's influence upon curricula in education at other universities, 201–203

Russell Sage Foundation, 94
Rutherford, Ernest, 77

Sachs, Julius, 197
Sadler, Sir M. E., 11, 64
Sage Foundation, 94
Saint John the Divine, Cathedral of, 214
Saint-Gaudens, Augustus, 211–213
Saint Gaudens, Reminiscences of, 212
Sallust, 76
San Francisco, 211
Saturday Evening Post, 209
Scholasticism, 121
School of Education, New York University, 59
School of Pedagogy, 195
Schools of Hellas, 118
Schurman, J. G., 11
Schwab, Charles M., 209
Science, British Association for the Advancement of, 227
Science in the nineteenth century, 76
Scientific spirit, 95, 171
"Scientific Use of the Imagination," 76–77
Scientist and Artist, 155–165:
Present-day exaltation of science, 157; importance of the artist's and the scientist's sharing each other's ideals, 158; the well-balanced combination in da Vinci, 159; how a physician may often experience the aesthetic pleasure of the artist, 161; need of coöperation of medical profession with other professions, 162; Gorgas's tribute to lay-professions, 163; the stimulative value of the needs of medicine to science, 164; how the selectiveness demanded of a physician makes him an artist, 164; tribute to the medical profession, 165
Scott, Professor Fred Newton, 126
Secondary Education, 7
Sermon on the Mount, 27
Sesqui-Centennial of the Declaration of Independence, 215, 217
Shakespeare, 191, 233
Shaw, Bernard, 233
Shaw monument, Boston, 212–213

A FEW REMARKS

Sherman group of St. Gaudens, 212–213
Sismondi, Jean C. L. S. de, 141
Sketch Book, The, 137
Smith, David Eugene, 197
Smith, Goldwin, 129
Snedden, Professor David, 198
Société des amis de l'Université de Paris, *Annales*, 113
Society and Solitude, 147
Society and Solitude, 145–154: Petrarch's *Life of Solitude*, 147; a liberal education found in a wide acquaintanceship with the masterworks of learning, 148; practical and spiritual values of occasional solitude, 148–149; contacts between student and teacher the supreme gift of college, 152–153; Petrarch on advantages of solitude with friends and literature, 153
Society of Mechanics and Tradesmen, General, address, to. *See* chapter XII
Solitude, Life of, 147
Solitude, values of, 148–149; Petrarch on, 153
Sons of the American Revolution, 104
Sophocles, 191
South, 186–187
South, The Advancing, 186
Southern Educational Review, The, 4
Spanish-American War, 189
Specialist in Higher Education, 12
Spencer, Herbert, 199, 231
Spinoza, Baruch, 231
Stanford University,
Stanley, Albert A., 126
State Normal School, Illinois, 6
Stevenson, Robert Louis, 55
Strayer, George, 198
Student body of an urban university, 104–105
Studies in Higher Education, 56
Sullivan, Louis H., 85
Supreme Court, U. S., 80
Suzzalo, Henry, 11, 198
Swing, David, 117

Taine, Hippolyte A., 30
Taft, William Howard, 11
Tanner, Professor Rollin H., 118
Teachers College, 195, 196
Ten Commandments, 27
Terence, 170
Terman, Professor Lewis M., 43
Testament of Beauty, 128
Tests, Army Mental, 44
Thinking, The Duty of, 183–191: Predilection of the majority for hastly negatives or affirmatives, 185; values in radicalism for conservatives and *vice versa*, 186; evidence of the revaluation of thinking by the South, 186; thought as wisdom rather than as logic, 187–188; importance of thinking in forestalling war, 189; use of the advances of science as material of thought, 190; use of ancient literatures as material of thought, 191
Thomas, George H., 181
Thompson, Boyce, Institute for Plant Research, 98
Thorndike, Professor Edward L., 197
Trinity College, Cambridge, 119
Truth, 124, 129, 130, 229
Tulane University, 4, 5
"Twain, Mark," 233
Tyndall, John, 76–77, 83

Unemployment, 45
United States Steel Corporation, 100
Universities: California, 7, 78, 211; Cambridge, 115, 119, 122; Chicago, 56, 58; Columbia, 197, *see also* Teachers College; Halle, 7; Illinois, 147; Johns Hopkins, 237; Liverpool, 74; London, 34, 122; Michigan, 5–7, 195; Minnesota, 55; Missouri, 5; North Carolina, 4; Ohio State, 56; Paris, 113–114; Purdue, 56; Tulane, 4, 5; Virginia, 223; Wisconsin, 190; Yale, 12, 57, 108, 237
University College, Oxford, 63, 66
University Heights, 3
University, The Idea of a, 99
University, urban, *See* Chapter IV *passim*
Urbanity, On, 91–114:

INDEX

Urban university molds sciences which in turn remold the city, 93; Advantages of coöperation between the municipal bureaus and the science departments of the university, and the necessity for both to be imbued with the scientific spirit, 93–95; relation of the urban university to the city school-system, 95; to agencies of social betterment, 97; to commerce and industry, 98; relationships between technical departments in industry and scientific departments in universities, 99; research in an urban graduate school, 101; the quality and needs of an undergraduate student body in an urban university, 103; the duty of the urban university to part-time and adult education, 106; the field of fine arts and letters in an urban university, 108; its duty to study municipal politics, 108–109; how it transcends group-consciousness, 111; its duty to combat materialism with ideals, 112

Vassar College, 103
Venable, President Francis P., 4
Vergerius, Peter Paulus, 75
Vergil, 76
da Vinci, Leonardo, 159–160
Victory, monument of, 212
Virginia, University of, 223

Vittorino da Feltre and other Humanist Educators, 74
Vocational Guidance, 48

Washington, D. C., 5, 12–14, 57, 207
Washington, Booker T., 42
Wendell, Professor Barrett, 126
Westminster Catechism, 27
Wheeler, President Benjamin I., 11
White, Stanford, 85
Whitehead, Professor A. N., 122, 123
Whitney, Professor William D., 237
Who's Who in America, 5, 51
Winchester, Professor C. T., 126
Wisconsin, University of, 190
Withers, Dean John W., 202
Wood, Professor Thomas D., 197
Woodberry, Professor George E., 126
Woodward, Professor William Harrison, 74
World Court, 190
World War, 34, 125, 163, 189
Wundt, Wilhelm M., 231

Yale Review, The, 87
Yale University, 12, 57, 108, 237
Yerkes, Robert M., 44
Yoakum, Clarence S., 44
Y. M. C. A. of Illinois, 6

Zeitlin, Professor Jacob, 147